THE COCKTAIL PARTY IS ENJOYING A RENAISSANCE

Unlike the all-night kegger or the eight-course sit-down meal, the cocktail party is elegant yet affordable, intimate but brief, and best of all, easy to prepare and a snap to clean up. Find out:

- What to say if a guest asks for *beer*
- What limit to set on the number of guests
- Why "no sitting" is a must—and how to rearrange your furniture
- How to calculate the right amount of hors d'oeuvres, drinks, and champagne (and what to keep on hand—just in case)
- Which background music is best (plus a list of suggested CDs and cassettes)
- What is so special about cocktail napkins—and why you cannot throw a party without them
- What works like a charm: for soft lighting, for a working bar, for storing guests' coats, for serving food and drinks—and much more

LESLIE BRENNER is a writer whose work has appeared in the *New York Times, New York* magazine, *Los Angeles Daily News, Harper's,* and *Food Arts.* She is also an accomplished cook, and co-author of *Essential Flavors* (Viking). She lives in New York City.

LESLIE BRENNER

THE ART OF THE COCKTAIL PARTY

THE COMPLETE GUIDE TO SOPHISTICATED ENTERTAINING

A PLUME BOOK

ILLUSTRATIONS BY
JULIET JACOBSON

PLUME

Published by the Penguin Group
Penguin Books USA Inc., 375 Hudson Street, New York, New York 10014, U.S.A.
Penguin Books Ltd, 27 Wrights Lane, London W8 5TZ, England
Penguin Books Australia Ltd, Ringwood, Victoria, Australia
Penguin Books Canada Ltd, 10 Alcorn Avenue, Toronto, Ontario, Canada M4V 3B2
Penguin Books (N.Z.) Ltd, 182–190 Wairau Road, Auckland 10, New Zealand

Penguin Books Ltd, Registered Offices:
Harmondsworth, Middlesex, England

First published by Plume,
an imprint of Dutton Signet,
a division of Penguin Books USA Inc.

First Printing, November, 1994
3   5   7   9   10   8   6   4   2

REGISTERED TRADEMARK—MARCA REGISTRADA

LIBRARY OF CONGRESS CATALOGING IN PUBLICATION DATA:
Brenner, Leslie.
The art of the cocktail party / Leslie Brenner : illustrations by
Juliet Jacobson.
p.   cm.
Includes bibliographical references.
ISBN 0-452-27235-1
1. Cocktail parties.   2. Appetizers.   3. Beverages.   I. Title.
TX731.B67   1994
642'.4—dc20   94–14395
                                                      CIP

Printed in the United States of America
Set in Garamond No. 3 and Copperplate 29ab and 32bc

Designed by Steven N. Stathakis

FOR THIERRY, WHO
CHEERFULLY SUFFERED
THROUGH THOUSANDS
OF HORS D'OEUVRES
INSTEAD OF DINNER.

☾

ACKNOWLEDGMENTS

The writing of this book would not have been possible without the help of a number of people who have been generous with their ideas, encouragement, advice, support, and palates, in varying combinations. Thank you to Michael Pietsch, Daniel J. Levy, An-My Lê and Chris Fodor, Janet Capron, Chris and Gina Russell, Erika Goldman, Jamie Alter, Michael Murdoch, Miri Abramis, Laura Fisher, John Brenner, my editor Ed Stackler, my agent Jennifer Rudolph Walsh, and especially, Juliet Jacobson.

CONTENTS

INTRODUCTION

"The chief virtue of cocktails is their informal quality. They loosen tongues and unbutton the reserves of the socially diffident." The waggish words of a Dorothy Parker or a G. B. Shaw? No—they're actually the opening sentences of the 1953 edition of that sturdy old Baedeker of the kitchen, the *Joy of Cooking.*

Indeed, for those among us who are the tiniest bit shy, and even those who aren't, it's hard to imagine facing a crowd of strangers at a party without a drink in hand. And if you drink, you need to eat—not a whole meal, but a *little* something. It was upon this basic principle that our most American of institutions, the cocktail party, was born.

Cocktail parties were a big part of my childhood—not because they happened in my parents' living room with any kind of great frequency, but because they seemed to me and my brothers the height of sophistication. We, as children, were excluded—required to stay in our rooms, presumably asleep, but sleep was always impossible when it sounded like adults on the other side of the double doors separating the kids' rooms from the rest of the house were having such a dandy time. To this day, the sound of ice clinking in a glass on the other side of any closed door induces in me a kind of Proustian swoon, the memories of wanting to grow up much more quickly than I was, a yearning to be an adult so I, too, could join in the gay chatter of cocktail parties, the unpleasant feeling of being left out of all the fun, all come rushing back to me. Now that I've passed the thirty-year mark and no longer wish to acknowledge, let alone *celebrate* my birthdays, I look back on that desire to leave childhood behind with mixed feelings: True, I have to pay bills now and worry about taxes whereas before I did not; but on the other hand, I *now get invited to cocktail parties*. And even better—I can *give* them.

And this has come about not a moment too soon—for cocktail parties are making a big comeback.

We didn't think of having them when we were in college—somehow they were too studied, not wild enough, completely inappropriate. We thought nothing of staying out until two or three or four in the morning at a party, the wilder the better. These were loud, raucous b.y.o.b.-type affairs, with dancing, alcohol, drugs, and superfluous snacks no more elaborate than chips, dips, and M&M's. Our bashes were inexpensive for the hosts, annoying to the neighbors. We had great stores of energy for such parties in those days, and in

the several years after we graduated; they were fun in the ni-
hilistic sense of the word, and the more people who showed
up, the merrier. We used to hope lots of people would crash,
adding to the festive setting, for the measure of a good party
was how large the crowd was. The next day we would awaken
after noon, hungover, dehydrated, vaguely depressed, only to
find cigarette butts ground into our rugs and red wine
soaked into our cushions.

Now we've grown up—sort of. As we've moved through
our twenties, perhaps into our thirties and beyond, we're still
social animals—we crave the company of others. Yet the
blowouts of our more youthful years no longer seem possible.

First of all, they're—how shall we say this?—
unbecoming.

Secondly, many of us now have children, or friends who
have to get home early enough so they won't have to take out
a second mortgage to pay their baby-sitter.

And thirdly, even if we are still among the very young
at heart whose motors are just warming up at midnight, we
might love to be invited to a late-night blowout, but nobody
in their right mind would want to *host* one. One might try
having a party called for nine o'clock. But in reality no one
ever shows up until ten-thirty, and it's hard to get people to
leave before one or two in the morning. Who would volun-
tarily offer up their home to such an unruly mob anymore,
especially when there's a good chance someone will throw up?

So what do we do, throw dinner parties? Of course
not! For most of us, they're far too expensive for a large
crowd. We might have a small one, but you only get to see

two or four of your friends that way. Sure, we could keep having them for all of our friends, but that would be labor-intensive, it would tie up our social calendar for months, and again—it would be incredibly expensive. Enter the cocktail party.

Emily Post, in her *Pocket Book of Etiquette,* sang their praises long ago, and her reasons for doing so still stand: "Cocktail parties are a popular form of entertainment. They require little preparation, are limited as to time, and you can entertain many more people at once in a small house." So right she is, and more so today than ever.

As a matter of fact, many of my friends tell me, "Leslie, we would love to throw a cocktail party. The problem is we don't have the first idea how!" So, pals o' mine, relax. There *is* an art to it, and a few tricks, but I'm going to walk you through the whole thing—from selecting a charming theme to mixing the perfect Rob Roy and passing hors d'oeuvres—with a healthy dose of the history of the cocktail party, famous and obscure cocktail party quotes and trivia, and even tips on being a good cocktail party guest along the way.

I've created the hors d'oeuvres in the book—and adapted the few that I've borrowed—expressly with the modern cocktail party in mind, and there are recipes for every level of skill, from those who think they can't boil an egg to expert cooks.

I've limited the number of cocktail recipes, sticking almost exclusively to the classics (they're classics for a reason), but adding a few standout newcomers. You'll also learn basic bartending technique (fear not—there's not much you need to know!) and the uses of arcane bar equipment such as cocktail shakers, martini pitchers, jiggers, and the like.

Nonimbibers will be happy to find a tempting assortment of out-of-the-ordinary nonalcoholic drinks as well.

All this so that this most swellegant of American traditions can be preserved, and passed on later to our children, and to their children after them. This way you, along with your friends and associates, can all be part of the renaissance of the cocktail party.

1

THE COCKTAIL PARTY
YESTERDAY AND TODAY

☾

Astonishing as it may seem, the cocktail party as a social institution has not been around very long at all. Born in the 1920s, the cocktail party is much newer than the cocktail itself, which dates all the way back to American revolutionary times. But ironically, it was during the Prohibition era that Americans really fell in *love* with cocktails.

Back in the nineteenth century, wine—usually in the form of Madeira—was popular with the smart set—though it was considered very unladylike to drink alcohol. In fact, it was even looked upon as ungentlemanly for a man who smelled even vaguely of brandy to appear in a lady's company! You can see how this kind of thinking might preclude the notion of a cocktail party.

In those days, for fun, people went to dinners and teas, and fancy types attended balls in the evenings. The favorite social activity, learned from European society, was the ritual of "calling" on people. To do this, one paid a social visit, calling card in hand, and kept track of where one stood in the social hierarchy according to whether one was received by the right people. After World War I parties became much more informal; while people no longer felt like going to balls, they did still want to visit one another at home. The Great War had knocked some of the pretension out of them, so the calling-card business started to fall by the wayside.

Meanwhile, the Temperance Movement, with its dreary puritanical pall, was gathering momentum. In 1920, the 18th Amendment to the Constitution put Prohibition into effect, making it illegal to manufacture or sell alcoholic beverages. But as it turned out, Prohibition didn't stop people from drinking at all—it merely changed *who* drank, *where* they drank, and *what* they drank, unwittingly laying the foundation for the birth of the cocktail party.

First of all, instead of drinking in saloons and restaurants, people now drank in speakeasies—and since alcohol was officially prohibited, Americans ditched Madeira in favor of stronger stuff (Make something illegal, and people want it more . . .). The speakeasies, competing for business, invented fanciful cocktails to lure the crowds—and they even welcomed women, who had never been allowed to drink in saloons. (Think of it—the cocktail party never could have been invented until women could drink!)

THE 15 MOST POPULAR COCKTAILS OF 1936

1. MARTINI COCKTAIL (DRY OR SWEET)
2. MANHATTAN COCKTAIL (DRY OR SWEET)
3. BRONX COCKTAIL (DRY OR SWEET)
4. OLD-FASHIONED WHISKEY COCKTAIL (SWEET)
5. SIDECAR COCKTAIL (SWEET)
6. CLOVER CLUB COCKTAIL (DRY)*
7. GIN RICKEY (DRY)
8. GIN FIZZ (SWEET OR DRY)
9. BACARDI COCKTAIL (DRY)
10. ALEXANDER COCKTAIL NO. 1 (SWEET)
11. ROCK AND RYE (SWEET)**
12. WHISKEY COCKTAIL (DRY)
13. SHERRY COCKTAIL (SWEET OR DRY)
14. DUBONNET COCKTAIL (SWEET)
15. CHAMPAGNE COCKTAIL

*Contained gin, vermouth, and a dash of yellow Chartreuse
**Rye whiskey with a piece of rock candy and the juice of a whole lemon

DO NOT GREET YOUR

GUESTS IN BARE FEET.

☾

During Prohibition, Americans had dozens of ingenious ways to keep themselves in liquor—including making it at home. This gave them the idea to *drink* it at home, which apparently they had never thought of before. In *Straight Up or On the Rocks: A Cultural History of American Drink,* author William Grimes writes:

> Suddenly, mixing a mean cocktail became one of the manly arts, like carving the holiday turkey. This new development set off a boom in the bar-accouterment industry. One magazine writer, strolling through a department store, noted that it sold twelve styles of silver cocktail glasses, twenty-three of glass, fourteen models of cocktail shakers, and eighteen kinds of hip flask . . . Some companies produced nonalcoholic Bronx, martini, and Manhattan cocktails, to which alcohol could be added.

Coincidentally, little tins of fancy foods—such as smoked oysters, olives, anchovies, and the like, the kind that happen to make tasty hors d'oeuvres—were now becoming widely available for the first time.

There they were—all the pieces in place. Drinks at home. Little tins of smoked fish. Fancy bar sets. Women finally allowed to drink with men. American sociability. *Poof!* By the end of the twenties, the cocktail party was born.

The heyday of the cocktail party was the 1950s, when much of the country enjoyed relative prosperity, a welcome relief after the Depression and then the war years. In *High Society,* the 1956 musical remake of *The Philadelphia Story,* Frank Sinatra and Bing Crosby duck out of a really swell cocktail party, into the library, with their glasses of champagne, for a moment of cocktail party appreciation and commemorate it with a Cole Porter song whose lyrics celebrate cocktail small talk; to this day, their musings still define cocktail-swell.

But their celebration of the cocktail party stands for something bigger: It's an expression that affirms the swellness of life.

Cocktail parties still enjoyed immense popularity in the early 1960s—which after all were really still the 1950s. Audrey Hepburn, in the guise of Holly Golightly, threw the greatest blowout cocktail party ever in the 1961 film *Breakfast at Tiffany's.*

But by the time the sixties hit, the cocktail party came to represent the Establishment and everything that the up-and-coming counterculture couldn't stand. So not too long after, the cocktail party took a little twenty-year sabbatical.

Sometime in the 1980s—that legendary decade of excess (just like the 1920s!), the smart set stopped turning up its nose at the cocktail party. In New York City today, cocktail parties have in fact staged a major comeback. Cocktail parties have long been popular both in the publishing business and in the art world; gallery openings and parties celebrating the publication of books are just about always cocktail parties. But the institution has caught on in such a big way that there's now plenty of crossover into the social setting.

What makes a cocktail party a cocktail party? Is it the host's impeccable attention to detail? The unfettered *joie de vivre* of the *bon vivant*? A certain *je ne sais quoi*? *Mais oui*—all three.

The best excuse for having a cocktail party is—no excuse at all. That way, you have the purest of all cocktail parties: the quintessential cocktail party, a cocktail party for cocktail party's sake.

By looking at some of the standard icons of the quintessential cocktail party, we can begin to understand its aesthetic: an uneasy balance of elegance and kitsch. Accordingly, every cocktail party cries out for certain signifiers—here are the top ten:

DO BE READY ON TIME.

☾

COCKTAIL DRESS

MARTINI GLASS

SWIZZLE STICK

PIMENTO-STUFFED OLIVE

COCKTAIL NAPKINS

MINGLING

TOOTHPICKS WITH FRILLY CELLOPHANE HATS

MARASCHINO CHERRY

CANAPÉS

ICE BUCKET AND TONGS

THE COCKTAIL DRESS

The cocktail dress holds a prominent place in the iconography of our entire culture, being, as far as I know, the only piece of clothing named after something to eat or drink (the tea-length skirt doesn't count, for it's the *length* that's named after a potation, not the garment). The cocktail dress's terse spiffiness reflects certain attributes of the cocktail party itself: Like the cocktail party, the cocktail dress is short, stylish, elegant, flirtatious, perhaps whimsical; and it reveals the personality of the wearer, just as the hors d'oeuvres reflect the personality of the host. Fashions may come and go, but the perennial cocktail dress simply puts one in the mood to go to a cocktail party.

THE COCKTAIL DRESS

MARTINI GLASS

As an icon, the martini glass holds a certain mystic power; it may be uniquely American, yet its stark, elegant outline is the international symbol for "cocktail," or "cocktail lounge," or "bar." It brings to mind a wide range of cultural associations, from Dean Martin to James Bond, usually masculine. One might think of it as the male counterpart to the cocktail dress. Although one *may* have a cocktail party without a martini glass, its presence places a definite seal on the ritual that is much to be desired. And as cool as it looks bearing the

MARTINI GLASS

11

cold clear elixir of a martini, one doesn't need to limit its use to the classic libation, either. Few cocktails are more visually striking than a ruby red Negroni (see page 225) filling up that infinitely mysterious yet reassuringly familiar isosceles shape, and it's hard not to feel elegant holding one.

SWIZZLE STICK

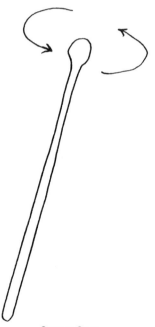

SWIZZLE STICK

Ask yourself honestly: How many times in your life have you used a real—not a flimsy plastic—swizzle stick? One sees them for sale in the pretty windows of fancy shops (but one never stops to buy), and one sees them in beautiful photographs of cocktails in food magazines and coffee table cocktail manuals. What are swizzle sticks? And what purpose do they serve?

Let's start with A) What are they? A swizzle stick is a straight glass rod, about five or six inches long, usually with a knob or a decorative element at one end. With few exceptions you don't actually *stir* a drink with it, for the drink already has been shaken or stirred. Yet there's something satisfying about removing it—more satisfying than if it hadn't been there at all. This brings us to B) What are they for? The truth is, they're for *removing*. They're a prop.

Will you use them? Perhaps not. Still, you need to have them at a cocktail party to add to the certain *je ne sais quoi*.

PIMENTO-STUFFED OLIVE

Ah, now *there's* an icon. Doesn't it just scream out "cocktail party"? Couldn't you just pop one into your mouth right now? In Barbara Kafka's encyclopedic *Party Food,* the author admits to liking the olives from other people's martinis so much that she offers a recipe for "Martini Olives." This *is* a marvelous idea, one I wish I had thought of, but oddly, Kafka calls for *olives with pits.* With pits! Why on earth, when one could have a pimento?

There's something about it that makes me swoon—a fat, green Spanish olive stuffed with a blood-red little wiggly pimento—it signifies all that is good and wholesome about cocktail parties. If you're not serving martinis, by all means slice up a few of these puppies and use them as a pretty garnish for canapés.

PIMENTO-STUFFED OLIVE

COCKTAIL NAPKINS

With the ritual passing of the hors d'oeuvre tray, the person passing clutches a couple inches' worth of cocktail napkins; it's up to the guest accepting the hors d'oeuvre to pluck a cocktail napkin. They're all-important, since *you don't have a fork.*

And over at the bar, you see a clever spiral of cocktail

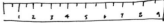

COCKTAIL NAPKIN

13

napkins there for the taking, ready to catch the refreshing condensation on the bottom of an old-fashioned glass.

I love them because they have only one *legitimate* use: the cocktail party. They're festive, they're fun, they're little, they're cute, they're square. Imagine—you're at a cocktail party, and someone has neglected this very important detail, and provided instead *dinner* napkins. *Quelle horreur!* Upon discovering the *faux pas* guests would become awkward and uncomfortable, and something ugly might even happen.

The cocktail napkin may be a vivid color and made of paper or it may be white and elegant and made of damask, or it may be a funky vintage linen model from the forties, or it may be the hilarious type one finds in old-style cocktail lounges, scribbled all over with stupid jokes or trivia quizzes. Only one thing is for certain: It is your friend. You *need* the cocktail napkin.

MINGLING

M I N G L I N G

"Excuse me, I should go mingle." The line is fabulous because it turns a snub into a social responsibility!

Mingling is the behavior that defines a cocktail party; it creates the lively chatter that, combined with the ice clinking in the glass and the background music, gives a cocktail party its auditory ambiance.

Mingling is the reason why we don't sit down at a cocktail party; we need to *mingle,* and that means having a short, upbeat conversation, and then moving around to the next.

Those of us who are shy may dread mingling, but fear not, for in Chapter 7 there are tips to aid the natural wallflowers, and help them become intrepid minglers.

TOOTHPICKS WITH FRILLY CELLOPHANE HATS

TOOTHPICK WITH FRILLY HAT

Wooden cocktail toothpicks with little cellophane hats in yellow, blue, red, and green are my favorite cocktail party signifier. From the time I was a small child, attracted by the bright cheerful cellophane, and fond of unraveling them slowly from the toothpick, they have always held a special place in my heart.

Pick them up in a party store—the ones I buy are "Cello Frills"—fifty to the pack in assorted colors. Spear a maraschino cherry with one, and you practically have a cocktail party right there.

MARASCHINO CHERRY

Spear one with a toothpick with a frilly cellophane hat, and you practically have a cocktail party right there.

For a while, in the 1970s and 1980s, maraschino cherries were out of vogue, thought of merely as limp little red things that oozed Red Dye #2 onto canned fruit salad.

15

MARASCHINO CHERRY

But they don't use Red Dye #2 in maraschino cherries anymore, and who eats canned fruit salad? Anyway, I never liked the kind of person who would self-righteously pluck the maraschino cherry garnish off a plate or out of a drink and delicately set it aside. I not only eat my own with considerable relish, I take theirs, too!

In fact, I'm a two-maraschinos-in-my-Manhattan type, so pretty and plump and cheerful are they.

Of course they *must* have stems; the kind without are utterly useless. Think of it: You can eat the stem!

Did you perchance ever wonder how people did that bar trick where they tie the stem of a maraschino cherry in their mouth without touching it with their fingers? *I'm going to tell you!* And you can amaze your friends with the trick at a cocktail party.

First, while no one is looking, take a maraschino cherry stem and tie it in a knot with your fingers. (Yes, *with your fingers!*) Now stick it in the back corner of your mouth.

Next, nonchalantly bring up the subject of tying maraschino stems with one's tongue, and inevitably someone will say they're sure it can't be done. "I can do it," you offer, casually. The person won't believe you, at which point you ask if they'd like to put five dollars on it. Someone will, so you take a new maraschino cherry, remove the stem, and put it in your mouth. With your mouth closed, your job is to root around with your tongue and find the one that's *already tied in a knot,* and bring it to the front of your mouth, and move the one that's not knotted to the back of your mouth. While it does require a little dexterity, it's *much* easier than tying one in a knot with your tongue, which as far as I know is impossible. And you don't even have to *act*, because you are doing some work to maneuver the two! Pull it out of your mouth, say *"Voilà,"* and you're five bucks richer.

CANAPÉS

First, let us define them, and get that out of the way. A canapé (pronounced *"ca-na-pay")* is any hors d'oeuvre that sits on a little piece of bread or a cracker or pastry. It could be anything from white bread with herb butter and shrimp to a tiny tart filled with chicken liver mousse. If bread is used, it is sometimes toasted (we no longer fry bread for canapés as they did in olden days), and most often spread with either a compound or flavored butter or another type of spread, then garnished with tasty tidbits. Sometimes they are hot—as Sardine Canapés, which are spread with a sardine paste and run under a broiler, and sometimes cold, such as Gravlax Canapés with Dill Sauce. (Recipes follow in Chapter 5.)

The reason they've earned a place as one of the top ten cocktail party signifiers is that they're gorgeous, jewel-like little morsels that both reveal the personality of the host and show the host's impeccable attention to detail. In a way the canapé is a cocktail party in microcosm.

Besides that, few can resist their cuteness, *and* the cocktail party is just about the only place one sees them.

CANAPÉ

"CAN O' PEAS, MY ASS—
THAT'S A RITZ CRACKER
WITH CHOPPED LIVER."
—FRANKIE PENTANGELI IN
THE GODFATHER, PART II

☾

ICE BUCKET AND TONGS

ICE BUCKET AND TONGS

Okay, I admit it: I *did* throw a cocktail party once without an Ice Bucket and Tongs. I just filled up a bowl with ice, and scooped out cubes with a spoon, but it was a really dumb idea, and there's nothing that looks less elegant. In any case, I'd never repeat the mistake.

Ice Bucket and Tongs come in a wide range of prices and tastes, from understated and elegant to overdone and gaudy, and from marvelously affordable to ridiculously expensive. The cost seems to have nothing to do with taste. A champagne bucket, by the way, is not an ice bucket—the chief difference being that an ice bucket has a lid, which is an important distinction, since we're trying to prevent our ice from melting prematurely.

So there you have the ten important cocktail party icons (more detailed information about how to use each of them follows in subsequent chapters). Supply them, and the rest—including the attitude of your guests—will follow. You'll see—any cocktail party that incorporates all of the top ten signifiers is *bound to succeed*.

And a lovely side effect of successful cocktail parties is that they're catching—before the evening is over, you'll hear from more than one guest who has suddenly decided that he, too, will have a cocktail party, and sooner rather than later. Your social calendar will rapidly fill up; you'll be busy for the next six months. Plus you'll have the unique satisfaction of knowing that you're the one who started it all!

Make your first cocktail party a classical one—the type we call the "Quintessential" (or "Swell") Cocktail Party. The opening pages of Chapter 2 explain what makes it "quintessential" and start you on your way. And then, after you host your first one (a smashing success, no doubt), you may decide to endow your next with a festive theme of some sort: Chapter 2 offers twenty-five snappy ideas. Or invent your own!

2

THE QUINTESSENTIAL (OR "SWELL") COCKTAIL PARTY AND VARIATIONS ON A THEME

Cocktail party signifiers aside, there are certain parameters you'll have to work within to achieve the Quintessential (or "Swell") Cocktail Party, and certain effects you'll want to strive for. Here's a little picture of what it looks like:

The party is called for 6:00 to 8:00 P.M., and your first guests arrive, she in a cocktail dress, he treading the fine line between casual and spiff, promptly at six. (Cocktail parties begin and end at the prescribed times.) Sparkly piano music plays softly on the stereo, lending a tinkling-piano-in-the-next-apartment feeling to your living room. Within the next fifteen minutes, at least half of the other guests arrive. Nobody is carrying flowers or wine; their only job is to show up looking smart, game for a fine time. Within a minute of their arrival, they'll have a drink in their hands, and hors d'oeuvres will soon be passed.

Your guests may select from a choice of two or three house cocktails, and two or three nonalcoholic drinks. More and more people are either twelve-stepping or cutting down on their alcohol intake for health reasons these days; plus, many of your guests will want to switch to something either nonalcoholic or with only a minute trace of alcohol after their first cocktail. Yet that doesn't mean they should be relegated to boring colas or club soda. That's why I've included an entire section—the second half of Chapter 5—on snappy new and classic nonalcoholic and low-alcohol drinks for you to choose from.

PASSING HORS D'OEUVRES

Your two or three house cocktails should be classic on-the-rocks or straight-up preparations; blender drinks are messy and undignified. Beer is frowned upon, at best. It simply doesn't belong at a cocktail party, and certainly not at a quintessential one. If someone asks for one, just wrinkle your nose, look quizzically at your guest, and say, "Beer?" as if you've never heard of it before. Then suggest one of your house cocktails.

First, let's discuss a technical point: the meaning of the word "cocktail." Food and beverage historians, writers, and linguists have argued long and hard about the origin of the word. In the most widely printed story, the widow of a Revolutionary War hero plucks out a tail feather from a rooster, stirs a drink with it, and exclaims, "Vive le cock tail!" An exhaustive rendition of this and other various theories can be found in William Grimes's book. As related by Grimes, an-

VIVE LE COCK TAIL

21

CHAMPAGNE COCKTAIL

other argues that the cocktail was invented by an Aztec nobleman who asked his daughter Xochitl (sounds like "cocktail") to deliver a drink to the king. My personal favorite is the one that credits Antoine Peychaud, the New Orleans apothecary who invented Peychaud's bitters and served them with brandy in egg cups (*coquetiers* in French). Even back in Revolutionary times English speakers had a devil of a time pronouncing French, so *coquetiers* became "cocktay" and then "cocktail."

In any case, it seems the matter will never be settled. But originally, the definition of a cocktail was that it contained a spirit, sugar, water, and bitters. *Technically* this is probably still true, if you consider that ice is water, yet bitters seems to be the ingredient that really defines a cocktail. With this in mind, it's easy to see why, for instance, an old-fashioned (bourbon or rye, water in the form of ice, a sugar cube, and Angostura bitters) is a cocktail. A champagne cocktail has champagne, a sugar cube, and bitters (though no ice, obviously). And also it seems one may use vermouth instead of bitters—giving us martinis, Manhattans, Rob Roys, and that entire family of cocktails. (One thing's for certain: a fruit cocktail is *not at all* a cocktail, nor is a shrimp cocktail, delicious as that may be.) In any case, there are plenty of so-called cocktails that aren't *technically* cocktails that one may serve at a cocktail party and still hold one's head high. In fact, many people use the terms "cocktail" and "mixed drink" interchangeably—as long as the drink contains a spirit, one seems to be on reasonably solid ground. For simplicity's sake, I'll take the liberty to play fast and loose with the word.

For the "Quintessential" (or "Swell") Cocktail Party, stick with the classics—the martini, the Manhattan, the old-fashioned, the gimlet, the daiquiri. Chapter 3 will tell you more specifically about how to choose. As for nonalcoholic beverages, the most classic of all is the Shirley Temple; the Virgin Mary is a distant second. For mineral-water drinkers, San Pellegrino water comes in tiny, shapely green glass bottles, which are much more elegant at a cocktail party than your run-of-the-mill Save-Rite Seltzer in the big plastic bottle (not the right mood at all!). San Pellegrino also makes fantastic flavored sodas in those same little bottles—the red one, called "Bitter," is sweet and bitter—you'd almost think you were drinking a Campari and soda! A Welsh company, Ty Nant Original Carbonated Natural Spring Water, offers its water in little cobalt blue bottles, which are so pretty that New Yorkers started using them for bud vases a couple of years ago—pretty damn *soigné,* too!

DO **NOT** DIP AN HORS

D'OEUVRE TWICE.

As for finger food, here I'll have to draw a line which some may see as rather too harsh. I strongly believe that plates do not belong at a cocktail party—not even little tiny plates. There's nothing more frustrating than trying to hold a drink with the left hand and a plate with the right hand, the cocktail napkin wrapped unattractively around the glass or crumpled pathetically underneath the plate, and a fork balanced precariously on top of the plate. With which hand is one supposed to pick up the fork? An old friend of mine named

Frank has conceived of an ingenious invention called a "necklace wineglass holder"—consisting of a strap that slings around one's neck and holds a wineglass upright in the middle of one's chest, leaving both hands free to manipulate hors d'oeuvres, or one hand to pick up a morsel and the other hand free to gesture. Would that I had had one recently when I was at a cocktail party at the Explorer's Club in New York. As I met a certain Australian cabinet minister, I tried to juggle a wineglass in my left hand while cradling my handbag in the crook of my right arm with a *small plate* of fish hors d'oeuvres and a fork balanced on top of my handbag. Forgetting myself for a moment, I reached to shake the minister's hand, and I watched in horror as the *small plate* of fish slid in slow motion off my handbag and onto the minister's foot.

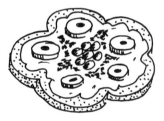

Such sloppy mishaps are by no means uncommon in these situations. The only remedy, and the kindest one to your guests, is to limit the hors d'oeuvres to true finger food—that is, small, self-contained tidbits that may be passed on a tray and eaten with one hand.

I'll even take it a step further and venture to say that finger food should be small enough to be eaten in *one* bite. Or *two* bites at the absolute most. It should not be too drippy or too crumbly or your guests will have a hard time looking elegant, and you'll have a mess on your hands.

The most classic cocktail party hors d'oeuvres are so classic they verge on cliché, but everyone loves them (that's why they're classic!). They are Chilled Shrimps with Cocktail Sauce (which disappear so fast, it's a joy to behold), Smoked Salmon Canapés, and meatballs. Luckily, I've provided recipes for all of them, including my special classic tangy cocktail sauce and "Modern Meatballs," which are much more delicious than those hard little dried-out meatballs of yesteryear. Round these out with either a Sardine Canapé or something with vegetables, such as Radishes with Anchovy Cream, or Endives with Gorgonzola and Walnut. You might want to have a dish or two of Spiced Almonds on hand as well.

In general, the important thing to remember with cocktail finger foods is that they should be *tasty*. Let "salty" and "spicy" be your watchwords. *Nuts???* you're thinking— *Cheese??? Butter???* Well, yes, you're absolutely right: The downside is that cocktail finger food usually isn't the healthiest food in the world—it tends to be high in fat and sodium. But neither are cocktails very healthy! If you take the attitude that *we don't eat this way very often,* surely we can indulge in the occasional salty, fatty, *tasty* cocktail snack, and make up for it by taking an extra lap around the track the next day. Look at it this way—in the nine months during which I created and tested the recipes in this book, I gained only ten pounds!

So there you have the Quintessential (or "Swell") Cocktail Party. Have a couple drinks, pass a few trays of hors d'oeuvres with frilly toothpicks, flirt a little, make some small talk, and before you know it, your guests will be on their way out, and you'll already be thinking about your next one.

Once you've mastered the Quintessential Cocktail Party, you'll be keen to try another variety—and the sooner the better! Here, then, are a few terrific ideas for *theme* cocktail par-

DO NOT RUMMAGE THROUGH YOUR HOST'S MEDICINE CHEST.

ties. Unless noted with an asterisk,* recipes for all hors d'oeuvres and drinks mentioned can be found in Chapters 4 and 5.

THE FÊTE

This is the cocktail party you throw in honor of someone: for your brother and his fiancée as an engagement party, for your cousin who has just returned from a year abroad, or your best friend who has just won a MacArthur "genius award." Anything goes food- and drink-wise; in a way, you can think of the theme literally as that person you're celebrating, and after that, just make the party as swell as possible.

- Order matches printed up with your honoree's name in really cheesy typeface—they are inexpensive, and well worth the comments they'll provoke.
- Make his or her favorite drink the house-special cocktail.
- Put up a banner that says "Congratulations so-and-so," or "Welcome back so-and-so," etc.
- Ask everybody to be really nice to the person you're honoring, for a change.
- If the fête is a bon voyage party, choose food and drinks that go with their destination. For instance, if your honoree is going to Hawaii or Japan, make it a Pacific Rim party (see below). If he or she is going to France, make it a Bas-

tille Day Party (see below); just don't call it that, and no one will be the wiser!

The beauty part of the fête is that it's really a multipurpose event, especially if you felt like throwing a cocktail party anyway, because at the same time you make big points with the person you're honoring, at little or no additional cost or effort!

ELBOW-LENGTH GLOVES

DIAMOND STUD EARRINGS

THE SOPHISTICATED
SOIRÉE

This special cocktail party, inspired by Nick and Nora Charles of *The Thin Man* movies, is basically your Quintessential Cocktail Party, but turned up a few notches on the elegance scale. If you really want to do it right, you should obtain a well-trained terrier like the Charles's crossword puzzle dog, Asta, and hire someone to sit at your grand piano and play Cole Porter tunes as background music. (It's best if your piano happens to be white. In fact, it's best if all your furniture is white, and your carpet, too.) On the other hand, if you've got an extra thirty-one thousand dollars burning a hole in your pocket, you'll certainly want to pick up one of Yamaha's new Disklaviers. It looks like a regular upright piano, and it may be played like one, but unlike a regular piano, every hammer is attached to a computer chip; you insert a diskette, and it will give you famous recording artists play-

BOW TIE

27

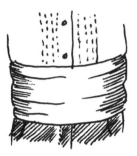

CUMMERBUND

CUFFLINKS

GLOVES

ing cocktail music on your piano! You can see the keys move, just like an old-fashioned player piano, but it's a thousand times more *sophistiqué* because it uses actual digital recordings of the artists.

For the Sophisticated Soirée, serve only the most *soigné* (French for "elegant") hors d'oeuvres—no sardines or anchovies! (No doubt you're beginning to see the difference between *classic* and *sophisticated.*) This is the evening for which you'll go all out—Caviar Bouchées, Scottish Smoked Salmon Canapés, Cherry Tomatoes Stuffed with Smoked Trout Mousse, canapés of *pâté de foie gras* (use the recipe for Pâté Rounds, and 86 the cornichons). As for the cocktails, there can't even be a question: martinis and champagne cocktails. They're clean, they're elegant, they're—well, they're *sophistiqué.*

Of course for the Sophisticated Soirée, you have to invite only your most elegant and debonair friends, and ask them, just this once, to *dress* for cocktails.

S O U T H - O F - T H E - B O R D E R
P A R T Y

Frank Sinatra once recorded a really stupid/great version of "Down by Mexico Way," and, when I was living in Los Angeles, the crazy guy who lived in the house in back of mine went through a phase where he would play it over and over again at top volume. All night long, we'd hear Frank singing, "Ay ay ay ay . . . ay ay ay ay. . . ." This is the feeling to strive for with the South-of-the-Border Cocktail Party.

Actually, musically speaking, you can do even better than Frank: use *real* Mexican music! There's tons of great mariachi music out there to give the perfect fiesta atmosphere, or if you want the perfect *retro-Mexicano* ambiance, try to find an old recording of Los Paraguayos from the fifties. Or anything by Herb Alpert and the Tijuana Brass (Herb Alpert may not be Mexican, but it *does* have the word "Tijuana" in it, and the brass sound is great for that South-of-the-Border ambiance).

Have the South-of-the-Border Party either on Cinco de Mayo (the fifth of May, for those who are unfamiliar with Mexican Independence Day), or on any day when it's warm enough that your guests can imagine they're transported to Cuernavaca or Cabo. Guests must still arrive in suitable cocktail attire, but they may top off their outfit with a sombrero, if they so desire.

The point of the South-of-the-Border Party, however, will be the finger food and drinks. Does a Margarita sound good right about now? A Tequila Sunrise? Difficult as it may be, *do not* give in to the urge to serve *cervezas,* however icy cold and delicious they may sound, and however well you think it might go with Shredded Pork Sopitas and Grilled Camarones. After all—it's not a *beer* party, is it? It's still a cocktail party you're after (and rightly so), or you wouldn't be reading this book!

As for the hors d'oeuvres, Mexican food *is* on the labor-intensive side. Sure, you can open a bag of tortilla chips and dump some salsa into a bowl, but really, how elegant is *that*? No, you'll have to put together some cute little *antojitos*. But relax—I've included elaborate—er, I mean *easy* step-by-step recipes, including my own homemade mini corn tortillas that are so remarkable *and* cute that I'm thinking of applying for a patent. These delectable *antojitos* are guaranteed to knock you right out of your *huaraches*. Choose from Regalitos, Shredded Pork Sopitas, Ceviche Tomatoes, Grilled Camarones, and Albondigas.

REGALITO

Meanwhile, here's an opportunity to really have some fun with decor, especially for our readers who live in California or Texas. Visit a local Mexican grocery, and pick up a dozen or so "miracle candles." These are the fabulous, colorful nine-inch-tall candles-in-glasses, charmingly decorated with decals of different *milagros* (miracles). In fact, though they're manufactured by Miracle Candle Company in Laredo, Texas, you can even find them, as I did, in towns as far-flung as New York! Maybe they even have them in Chicago! Just look in your local Hispanic grocery or even Caribbean "botanica." I have "San Miguel Archangel" in red, "La Milagrosa" in blue, "Siete Potencias Africanas" (Seven African Powers) in *rainbow* colors, and my all-time favorite, "La Mano Poderosa" (The Powerful Hand) in green. Collect all ten!

If you happen to have a *serape* lying around (who doesn't?), by all means drape it over a card table and set up your bar on it, and for cocktail napkins go to a party shop in a Hispanic neighborhood and pick up some cute ones with Spanish-language jokes on them.

BASTILLE DAY PARTY

Here's your chance to show off your French cooking, language skills, if any, and share with your friends a healthy dose of *Liberté, Fraternité,* and *Egalité.* Actually, the French don't even call Bastille Day "Bastille Day"; they call their Independence Day "Quatorze Juillet," just as we don't call our Independence Day "Independence Day," we call it "The Fourth of July."

But never mind about that. For the Bastille Day Party, you'll want to decorate your living room in red, white, and blue; if you hunt around the party shop, you may even be able to find some little French flags. Place little votive candles in small glasses around the room to add *ambiance.*

For music, Edith Piaf would be perfect, or look for a contemporary French gypsy-jazz guitarist named Christian Escoudé—try his recent CD, *Holiday.* Or any cheesy French music, especially if it features an accordion. In fact, there's a whole accordion music genre in French called *Valse Musette,* which is their cultural equivalent to country-western music. Aimable (his whole name—I guess he's like a French male Cher) and André Vershuren both have high cheese content. Or look for something by Yvette Horner, who's a cross between Edith Piaf and Dolly Parton.

As far as finger food goes, you happen to be in luck, for

31

the hors d'oeuvres in Chapter 3 that happen to be French are the best to be found anywhere. And why not? Don't forget, *hors d'oeuvre* is a French word! Choose from Leek Barquettes, Gruyère Puffs, Crispy Ham and Asparagus Rolls, Pissaladiettes, Canapés Niçoises, Pâté Rounds with Cornichons, and Mushroom Barquettes.

Delightful apéritifs may replace regular cocktails at the Bastille Day Cocktail Party; in fact the French really have the right idea in this respect. In French culture, the apéritif, usually either a type of vermouth (which is a fortified wine) or a *pastis* (any one of a number of anise-flavored drinks) is designed to allow people (in this case the French) to mark the transition from day to evening with a little relaxing drink. Lillet, a sweet, white vermouthlike drink, is lovely and refreshing, traditionally garnished with a slice of orange. Dry white vermouth livened up with a drop of cassis is also yummy. Pernod is an elegant *pastis;* serve it straight up, and leave pitchers of ice water around for people to add to their taste. When you pour in the water, the Pernod suddenly turns cloudy. Or, if you want to go for more of a *Wages of Fear*–French-truck-driver effect, serve Ricard instead of Pernod, also with pitchers of water.

For toasting, replace "Down the hatch" with *"À votre santé,"* or, if you're more intimate, *"À la tienne"* (here's to yours). Or, if you should happen to be toasting someone named Stephen, say *"À la tienne, Etienne."* If there is a French person in the room, he'll find this *amusant.*

FOURTH OF JULY PARTY

Okay, we *had* to get this over with, but you knew it was coming. But seriously, what better thing to do before going to see fireworks, which usually start at nine o'clock, than *having a cocktail party*?! Make this one a festive outdoors affair, if you can, but no sloppy barbecues for us. Think of this as an All-American cocktail party. If you're staying indoors, order a bunch of helium balloons in red, white, and blue, and let them float up to your ceiling. Party shops are chock-full of Fourth of July decorations, so buy a bunch of American flags, and stick them in your houseplants, or outdoors in the garden. The patriotic possibilities are endless.

Try a luscious summertime menu of Firecracker Endives, Mini Ham and Cheddar Biscuits, Barbecue Chicken Drumettes (listed as a variation of Tiki Drumettes), and Potato Puffs.

For cocktails, how about Watermelon Martinis, Blueberry Martinis, and old-fashioneds, and for the alcohol-free zone, refreshing Lemon Twist?

BLACK AND WHITE PARTY

Black ingredients—caviar, truffles—tend toward the pricey, so the Black and White Cocktail Party can be a tad expensive. If you can swing it, though, it ranks way up there with

33

the Sophisticated Soirée on the *soigné* scale. In any case, there are a few lower-cost options among the following possibilities: Caviar Bouchées (with crème fraîche), Black and White Caviar Canapés, Creme Cheese and Black Olive Canapés (use recipe for Cream Cheese and Olive Canapés, and substitute canned black olives for the green ones), Chèvre and Shaved Truffle Tartlets*, Black and White Potato Puffs (make plain Potato Puffs and add before piping a crumpled-up sheet or two of *nori*—black Japanese seaweed—for eye-catching black specks).

For cocktails, serve martinis garnished with a cocktail onion and a black olive (the kind that comes in a can, not a marinated one), and Johnnie Walker Black Label on the rocks, mineral water, and blackberry or black cherry soda.

- Use tablecloths and cocktail napkins in black and white design, or use half black cocktail napkins and half white.
- Ask your guests to attire themselves in black and white—tuxedos get extra points.
- Invite all the newspaper reporters and editors you know.
- Invite anyone you know whose last name is either Black or White.
- Invite African-Americans and whites in equal numbers and arrange yourselves in a checkerboard pattern as a party stunt.
- Feature the music of black and white recording artists.

*Recipe not included

BLUE HAWAII PARTY

Find some really cheesy Don Ho–type music, heavy on the ukuleles, and pretend your living room is the inside of Trader Vic's. As guests enter, ceremoniously place leis around their necks, and kiss them on both cheeks. This is a really good theme party to have as a bon voyage party for someone who's going to Hawaii, because you can cover up your envy by making fun of the whole thing.

Plus it's a chance for you to show off your drink-garnishing skills. Of course you mustn't pass up Guy's Blue Hawaii, which is perhaps the single most festive drink in the book. Mai Tais, Zombies*, and Happy Daves go nicely, too.

Actually, even though these island-type drinks can be very alcoholic, you can create some wonderful nonalcoholic tropical drinks, too. My favorite is the Virgin Dave (which is the nonalcoholic version of the Happy Dave, which I named after my brother). In any case, go heavy on the fruit garnishes, getting as wild as you want with pineapples, coconut slices, mango slices, and maraschino cherries, which, though they aren't exactly tropical, do leave an appealing little red spot on other fruits that are.

And best of all, you can pass pupu platters! "Pupu" is simply Hawaiian for "appetizer"; fill large serving platters with assortments of Coconut Shrimp, Tiki Drumettes, and

*Recipe not included

Sweet and Sour Meatballs, all interspersed with chunks of pineapple speared on cocktail toothpicks with frilly cellophane hats. Place small bowls of macadamia nuts here and there for that island touch.

ST. PADDY'S DAY COCKTAIL PARTY

Guests must wear green or they get pinched. The food isn't very intriguing at this particular party, so no need to worry about your guests overstaying their welcome. As befitting the holiday, drinks are the real focus, and green or green-tasting they must be. Try gimlets or daiquiris, or buckle down and pour Irish whiskey, even if it's not green. *You'll* be green the next day. Corned Beef and Cabbage Canapés were created specially for this holiday; serve them with Potato Puffs.

BALI HAI PARTY

This is suspiciously similar to the Blue Hawaii party— though it's Polynesian. Serve pupu platters and Mai Tais. In fact, you can use the same drinks, same garnishes, same pupus, or, if you like, any of the French finger food, since Polynesia is a French territory. The effect you want to go for musically is the distant beat of tom-tom drums, sort of menacing yet alluring. Look for any Tahitian music—it's amazingly uplifting, and anything you find will probably be wonderfully and instantly put people in a party mood.

VALENTINE'S DAY COCKTAIL PARTY

Decorate your home with red roses and valentine hearts, and place little bowls of "conversation hearts" (the candies that say things like "YOU'RE SWELL" and "BE MINE") here and there. Invite lovers and loveable single people you want to fix up with each other.

Serve red and white Potato Puffs (plain and sun-dried tomato) and assorted canapés cut out with a heart-shaped cookie cutter. At the bar: pink ladies, martinis, and Campari and tonics.

GATSBY PARTY

FLAPPER DRESS

- Invite the richest people you know—everyone else has to come as a "flapper." This has to be a *large* party, as "They're so intimate."
- Serve two kinds of stuffed eggs: Stuffed East Eggs* and Stuffed West Eggs.*
- Serve Long Island Iced Tea.*
- Play jazz-age jazz (for an anthology CD, look for *The Jazz Age: New York in the Twenties,* on the Bluebird label).
- Fill your bathtub full of gin, and dance in it.

*Recipe not included

COMMUNIST PARTY

At this nostalgic romp into the good old days of the Cold War, guests should wear red, and call each other "Comrade." Serve shots of Stolichnaya, room temperature, and no fancy-schmancy flavorings. Caviar and Blinis,* Creamed Herring and Beet Canapés, Shrimp Canapés, and Cucumber Cups with Smoked Whitefish Mousse.

Play all your favorite balalaika hits.

DO REUSE A TOOTHPICK.

FLYIN' DOWN TO RIO PARTY

With this festive Brazilian-theme party, cachaça—Brazilian sugarcane liquor—is the star. Serve it with a number of different yummy fruit juices—passion fruit, coconut cream and lime, pineapple, with or without a dash of egg white to turn the drink into a creamy *batida* (see Chapter 5 for more ideas). And of course there's the Caipirinah—a lime-y knockout of a Brazilian cocktail.

For hors d'oeuvres, Island Crab Bouchées, Stamp 'n' Go (although it's not called that in Brazil), and Shrimp and Hearts of Palm Empanadas.

For music, look for anything by Antonio Carlos Jobim

or Milton Nascimento, *Brasileiro* by Sergio Mendes, and a Verve anthology called *Samba Brasil*.

Dress 1930s Hollywood Brazilian—in fact, if you feel like piling fruit on your head, so much the better!

CARIBBEAN PARTY

This is a cocktail party with an island beat—rumba, zouk, Afro-Cuban, merengue, reggae, steel band music, soca, salsa. Mario Bauzá's *My Time Is Now* and the vintage *Tremendo Cumban,* by Machito and his Afro-Cuban Orchestra, are snappy for starters. Why, you might have so much fun with just the music, you won't need any food and drink! But if you should desire a little something, Bompi's Punch, piña coladas, and daiquiris ought to make your guests wiggle their hips suggestively.

You can borrow any of the finger food from the Flyin' Down to Rio cocktail party, but you simply *must* have the Caribbean staple—Stamp 'n' Go, plus Coconut Shrimp and Jerk Drumettes.

BOMPI'S PUNCH

CHRISTMAS COCKTAIL PARTY

Everyone loves a Holiday Cocktail Party a week or two before Christmas; after all, it's the height of the cocktail party season! I find Scotch to be particularly cozy this time of year—who would kick a Rob Roy and a Chicken Liver Mousse Canapé out of bed? Mushroom Barquettes and Endives with Gorgonzola and Walnut round out the menu—and Caviar Potato Pancakes* would provide a nice nod to Hanukkah. You can even make a big bowl of Hot Buttered Rum. (Eggnog, while delicious, can be a little heavy on the palate with hors d'oeuvres.)

Select really cheesy Christmas music, such as the Elvis Christmas CD. Other CD anthologies are available seasonally.

Be sure to have your tree up and decorated (if you're the type), and use pine boughs lavishly to adorn your walls—they'll make your home smell heavenly. Red and green candles complete the holiday feeling.

R E T R O   C O C K T A I L   P A R T Y

RADISH ROSES

The Retro Cocktail Party celebrates the glory days of the cocktail party, the days when the martini was king, and people actually put lampshades on their heads instead of just threatening to.

Pass Cream Cheese and Olive Canapés, Rumaki,* Modern Meatballs, Radish Roses* or Radishes with Anchovy Cream, Cheese Balls Rolled in Nuts,* and Stuffed Celery Gems and pour martinis, Manhattans, and Shirley Temples. Dress fifties kitsch. For music, dig up some swingin' old Louis Prima and Keely Smith, Frank Sinatra, and Nat King Cole.

*Recipe not included

POLITICALLY CORRECT COCKTAIL PARTY

Use reusable glass only and cloth napkins, serve hors d'oeuvres made only from products grown by sustainable agricultural methods, and lots of freshly squeezed vegetable juice drinks, and make sure any liquors you pour aren't from countries that torture political prisoners. Decorate your living room to look like a rain forest, assign someone to be the word police or language monitor, and invite your most politically aware friends. Oh, and have a girl be the bartender.

GRAND OLD PARTY

Do it like the *real* Republicans do—have a "Grand Old Party" with Cheese Whiz on Ritz crackers,* cocktail weenies on toothpicks with frilly red and blue cellophane hats,* and martinis all around. Everyone must wear red, white, and blue polyester and complain about social programs and reverse discrimination. The best time for the Grand Old Party is during a Republican Convention—turn on the TV instead of background music!

PLANTATION PARTY

DO NOT SCARF DOWN TOO
MANY HORS D'OEUVRES.

If it's warm out and you have a screened-in porch, you can't *not* have this party. Wear starchy white linen, Panama hats, and billowy cotton dresses with wide-brimmed hats, and go on ahead and treat your guests to Mint Juleps (sip 'em nice 'n' slow), Planter's Punch, Mini Ham and Cheddar Biscuits, Chilled Shrimp with Cocktail Sauce, and Corn and Sage Beignets.

THIRD WORLD COCKTAIL PARTY

Okay, maybe it's a contradiction in terms, but think of it: world music, cool duds from developing nations, and the snappiest hors d'oeuvres from around the globe: Curried Cashews, Stamp 'n' Go, Sopitas or Regalitos, and An-My's Summer Rolls. Wash 'em down with Caipirinahs, Margaritas, and Cuba Libres.

PACIFIC RIM PARTY

Lots of possibilities here—for your guests may dress in Hawaiian shirts or kimonos, or even Seattle hippie or California cool! Get seven CDs—Japanese koto music, Tahitian drums, Balinese gamalan music, Chinese opera, mariachi, Australian didgereedoo and Peruvian pipes. No one will be entirely happy with it, but it'll be so *interesting*!

For hors d'oeuvres, what could be better than Shrimp Toast, Tiki Drumettes, Grilled Ginger-Lime Shrimp, Sushi,* and An-My's Summer Rolls? Pour Orange Flowers, Singapore Slings, Guy's Blue Hawaii, Virgin Daves, and Creamy Coco-Carrot Specials.

NEW YEAR'S COCKTAIL PARTY

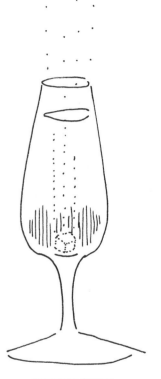

CHAMPAGNE COCKTAIL

Have this one either on December 31, to help people warm up for New Year's Eve, or on January 1st, as a hair-of-the-dog-that-bit-them the night before. Champagne cocktails, Bloody Marys, Martinis au Kurant, and Caviar Bouchées, Gruyère Puffs, and Smoked Salmon Canapés.

COLUMBUS DAY—OR PICK A FEAST DAY—PARTY

The operative idea is Italian. It can really be any time of the year, since every day is the feast day of some saint or other. Decorate in red, white, and green crepe paper and string up carnival lights.

43

Pass Red, White, and Green Potato Puffs (flavored with roast garlic, basil, and sun-dried tomato), Mozzarella Bites, Rosemary Grilled Shrimp, and Prosciutto and Melon with Port Sauce. Put little baskets of Parmesan Straws on your end tables. And make them a cocktail they can't refuse: Negroni, Traditional Martini (using Cinzano vermouth, of course), Peach Bellini, or Bianco Cocktail. Don't forget the San Pellegrino water and Pellegrino Bitter.

N O R T H   S E A   P A R T Y

This is the Scandinavian smorgasbord of cocktail parties, and a great chance for you to show off your gravlax, which everyone always thinks is incredibly impressive even though it's easy. So, then, Gravlax Canapés, Shrimp Canapés (garnish with dill), Cucumber Gems, Creamed Herring and Beet Canapés, and Endives with Danish Blue and Walnuts (use recipe for Endives with Gorgonzola, and substitute Danish Blue). Complement them with that very Scandinavian cocktail the Aurora Borealis (okay, it was invented in New York, but it *does* feature Aquavit)—or, for that matter, you might want to serve ice-cold Aquavit poured all the way to the top of little cordial glasses.

O O 7   P A R T Y

This is surely the dumbest idea I've had, yet no doubt it will be popular. The only drinks: vodka martini, very cold, very dry, stirred, not shaken. The girls you invite (don't invite any real women) must be tall, beautiful, voluptuous, and show a lot of cleavage. There is actually a two-CD set out called *The Best of James Bond: 30th Anniversary Limited Edition,* which is music from all the James Bond films. Invite Sean Connery, Roger Moore, and Tim Dalton. Probably they'll be busy— but wouldn't it be amazing if one of them showed up? You never know! And here's the time to display all the gadgets you've collected over the years from the Sharper Image catalog—you can pretend you're Q!

3

PLANNING

YOUR PARTY

Now, before you go any further, go out to a party supply store and purchase a little bag of cocktail toothpicks. These cocktail party icons will put you in a swell mood, and provide exactly the right aesthetic to get your juices flowing. Now go home, mix a martini, spear an olive or two with a cocktail toothpick in your favorite color (though I wouldn't suggest green, because it won't look good with the olive. Unless of course you decide on a Gibson instead—because the green cellophane shows up nicely against the nice white cocktail onion), drop the garnish in the glass, and there—doesn't it look festive? Next grab a pad and pencil, and we're ready to begin the planning.

Fortunately for you, a cocktail party is the easiest thing in the world to plan. (Executing it is another matter entirely, but more about that in the next chapter.) The first thing you must decide is whether you want to have a party with a theme, or simply the Quintessential "Swell" Cocktail Party. Let's, for simplicity's sake, opt for the "swell" party. You already have your toothpicks, so you're practically halfway there. (If, on the other hand, you'd prefer a theme, refer back to Chapter 2 for an inspirational array of choices.)

W H O M   T O   I N V I T E

How many people constitute a cocktail party?

Twelve. If you have ten, it's not a full-fledged cocktail party; it's really just having a few friends over for drinks. Which is nice, too, don't get me wrong; only it's not a cocktail party. And mind you, twelve only constitutes a quorum if your space is exceedingly small, like mine. If you have a normal-size living room and only ten guests, it will appear that they're floating about too freely, like so many molecules in search of an organism. It simply won't do.

A cocktail party is meant to be an intimate gathering, so do confine it, if possible, to one room. If you have a really large room, thirty is a reasonable maximum. But understand that if you choose to have that many, you'll be spending more time than you might like cutting the crusts off of sandwich loaves for your canapés. But you do want to have enough people so they fill up the room to a reasonable degree. This provides for a festive atmosphere, and also lets you avoid the appearance that nobody showed up.

"A COCKTAIL PARTY IS A
PUBLIC THING. YOU INVITE
PEOPLE TO A COCKTAIL
PARTY."

—A. R. GURNEY,
THE COCKTAIL HOUR

☾

The rule for counting probable attendees is different than for most parties, where one can only expect two-thirds of those invited to attend. Your return on a cocktail party will be much higher—you may lose one or two invitees who'll be out of town (won't they be sorry!), but everyone else who's around surely will want to attend. For all the world loves a cocktail party! And why shouldn't they? Your guests are given fabulous drinks, cute little hors d'oeuvres, and they don't even have to stay too long.

Look at this as a great opportunity to invite people to whom you owe an invitation because they've invited you so many times for dinner, even though Emily Post vehemently disagrees with me on this point. Invite business contacts you've been trying to figure out how to schmooze, even if it sounds Machiavellian. Or, if you're unattached, invite attractive members of the opposite sex with whom you'd like to ingratiate yourself under the acceptable and innocuous umbrella of a social gathering. For many such social dividends, a cocktail party is a perfect excuse. And of course invite your friends—a few old and a few new—or you won't have any fun.

Remember, though, that all your guests will have to converse with one another. It's good to have a healthy mix of people who are acquainted and those who aren't, business people and friends, single people and couples. Invite a good conversationalist or two, even if you're not crazy about them—they'll keep things lively. Try to minimize the bores. Think of what people might have in common—for instance, two graphic designers who've never met will have plenty to talk about. So will two physical therapists. Or two farm-hands.

And do consider your single friends—you can even look at this as an opportunity to play matchmaker without being obvious. If you're inviting three single men, be sure to invite a few single women. Look at it this way—if it appears that two singles hit it off, everyone else will have something to whisper about. And if something great comes of it, they'll be beholden to you for the rest of their lives (or at least the duration of their relationship).

Think about potential problems and conflicts between different personalities. If you happen to know that X and Y can't stand each other, don't invite both of them—usually there's not enough room to get lost in the crowd at a cocktail party. And if Jane is having an affair with Jill's husband, don't invite Jane! (Or don't invite Jill, depending on your sense of moral rectitude or humor.)

Don't invite too many coworkers, or shoptalk will take over. And remember that if you invite some, others will hear about it and be insulted that they weren't invited. If all this is beginning to sound like a giant headache, you can always change your mind, forget about the party, and use the money you save to go out to a fabulous dinner instead.

SETTING A DATE

You'll want to invite people about two weeks in advance, but first you'll need a couple days to put everything together, and a few days just to let everything sink in, so choose a date at least three weeks from now, and probably a little more. Now take out a calendar and look at it. Are there any major holidays around the date you have in mind? This can be good or bad. It can be bad if it's a holiday for which people tend to leave town, which varies from city to city and town to town. For instance, New Yorkers all leave the city for Memorial Day, but Angelenos don't. Holiday proximity can be good if there's somebody you know will *expect* an invitation but whom you don't really want to invite, and you happen to know that person will be going out of town for that particular holiday. Then you can invite that person and not have to suffer their presence in your home! Of course there is a slight possibility that this could backfire, and the person might decide that your cocktail party sounds so intriguing, so fabulous, so—*unmissable*—that they'll cancel their trip. Anyway, it's a risk.

DO HAVE PLENTY OF EXTRA ICE ON HAND.

☾

On the other hand, you may decide to have a theme party that coincides with a holiday, such as a South-of-the-Border Party for Cinco de Mayo, or a Bastille Day Party, or a Valentine's Day Party, and so forth.

Once you've got the week narrowed down, you'll have to commit to a day of the week.

Weekdays hold certain advantages over weekends. For one thing, if it's a "school night," people are grateful to get home early anyway. They can come directly from work, have a drink and a nibble, chitchat a bit, and then go home to dinner and their real life, and the whole thing has just been a little bright spot in an otherwise ordinary day. The downside of the weekday cocktail party is that if, like most of us, the host has a job, a weekday is virtually impossible—unless he or she takes a day off from work—or possibly an afternoon—the day of the party in order to prepare.

If you do choose a weekday, the best is Friday, since people are in the mood to start cutting loose a little after the workweek, yet they're still in the rhythm of the workweek, so they won't cut *too* loose and stay longer than they're supposed to. The beautiful thing about a cocktail party is that since it is early and lasts only two hours or so, guests can still make an appearance even if they have other plans for the evening.

Thursdays are also a lovely choice. Usually people are in a terrible mood on Monday, so that's not a great choice; Tuesdays and Wednesdays are okay in a pinch.

As for the weekends, the obvious advantage is that you can have the whole day guilt-free to stay home and prepare for the party. Yet weekends are a little too—how should we put it—*relaxed* in mood; cocktail parties depend on nervous energy for their punch. Sunday might be a good choice, because people start to get a little tense thinking about the workweek ahead, so that a cocktail party is just the thing to loosen them up. Saturday can be nice in its way, especially if people have tickets to something, or a dinner invitation for later in the evening. The problem with Saturday is if people were just maybe thinking of going to dinner or a movie after they leave your cocktail party, they're the types who wind up overstaying their welcome, trying to make a dinner out of hors d'oeuvres! However, if you're loud and clear on the issue

☾

of the duration of the party when you extend the invitations, this shouldn't be too much of a problem. In the old days, people used to have a "supper" after the cocktail party to which only certain people were asked to stay after the party. Isn't that *barbaric*! I can think of nothing more insulting than knowing that while others have been invited to stay on to supper, I have not.

So, decide on a weekday or weekend, check for proximity of holidays, and pick a date. That wasn't so bad, was it?

INVITATIONS

It's not necessary to send written invitations, unless you're fêting someone (then they can save the invitation and put it in their scrapbook or whatever), or you want to make a huge point of a special theme. Here, Emily Post and I agree: telephone calls are fine.

On the other hand, people do tend to take the RSVP more seriously if written invitations have been sent—and therefore incidences of no-shows will be lessened.

Either way, whether you opt to send written invitations or use the phone, do be sure—and this is extremely important—to specify the times—for example, 5:30 to 7:30 P.M., or 6:00 to 8:00 P.M. Which brings us to Cocktail Party Rule #1.

RULE #1: A COCKTAIL PARTY IS NOT A DINNER PARTY.

The proper time for a cocktail party is a two-hour slot *before* dinner, so your guests *must* absolutely understand that they're not to expect a meal! So probably you should repeat the times, at least twice, so they can get it through their thick heads that this is not a dinner invitation. Don't be afraid to be incredibly obvious and brazen, and say something like, "The cocktail party is from six to eight, Dottie, and by the way, I'd be surprised if you didn't bump into someone there you'll wind up going out to dinner with after!" The other alternative is to pretend you have something to go to afterward, and say, "The cocktail party will be from five-thirty to seven-thirty, and unfortunately, Dottie, we can't join you for dinner afterward—we're invited out."

Two hours is the correct duration for the cocktail party. Think of the starting time as actual—unlike a late-evening party, where you call it for nine, and people start showing up at eleven, a cocktail party begins promptly. It's one of the few occasions where "fashionably late" is decidedly unfashionable. Guests *may* arrive late, and still remain comfortably within the bounds of etiquette, but they also *must* leave on time. When you start to get sick of the whole affair, put away the drinks, and your guests will go away. And while you want to be sure to have *enough* hors d'oeuvres, do not make the mistake of having too many hors d'oeuvres: the guests should still be hungry enough to require dinner, thus forcing them out the door eventually.

A SELECTION OF HORS
D'OEUVRES SERVED AT
A DINNER GIVEN BY
THE NEW YORK
ENTOMOLOGICAL
SOCIETY

DUSTED OVEN-CRUNCHY CRICKETS
POPPED WAXWORMS
INSECT AND AVOCADO CALIFORNIA
ROLLS
WITH TAMARI DIPPING SAUCE
MEALWORM BALLS IN ZESTY TOMATO
SAUCE
WAXWORM FRITTERS WITH PLUM
SAUCE

☾

If you decide, for whatever reason, to send out written invitations, for heaven's sake don't go hunting for them in a Hallmark shop—you'll wind up with invitations that are the wrong kind of cheesy. Find something as understated as possible. Of course the best thing to do is to have them printed up; my friend Felix does really nice ones right on his computer, using a layout program like Pagemaker and printing them on thick, creamy paper.

And a new innovation in party etiquette is the faxed response. To execute this clever move, just put "RSVP," then your phone number, then your fax number. The reason this is so nifty, is it solves the potential problem of what happens if people don't really feel like chatting with you when they call to respond—if for instance they don't know you, they're shy, they're overburdened with work, or they don't want to make excuses why they can't show up for a measly little two-hour affair. In any of these cases, the responding party can always hope to get your answering machine, and just leave a message, but what if you're one of those people who works at home or who always picks up? The fax option saves everyone a lot of embarrassment; plus it's fun!

Inevitably, there will be some well-meaning sap who asks if he or she can bring something. Discourage this, because it's *just not done*! First of all, since you're not even giving them dinner, they don't "owe" it to you, and second of all, what could they possibly bring you that would help you—unless, of course, it's their butler who doubles as a bartender. To get out of this gracefully, just tell the person, "Of course not, silly, but thank you for asking." Be sure to include the "silly"; if you don't, there's always a danger that they'll just think you're being polite.

If this is all sounding too persnickety, pour yourself another martini, insert a fresh "cello frill" into a fresh olive, and you'll feel rejuvenated. Or not.

AND WHAT ABOUT CHILDREN?

A simple, resounding "no." (See Rule #2, below.)

RULE #2: COCKTAIL PARTIES ARE *NOT* FOR CHILDREN.

First of all, it's not cute to see children mixing drinks or passing trays of hors d'oeuvres, and it's certainly not cute seeing children taking a sip of some hilarious adult's martini. Second of all, the cocktail party is simply not a children's event. It's a time to act sophisticated, or stupid, but stupid in a decidedly unchildlike way; it's maybe a time to flirt (not the most wholesome thing for children to witness), maybe a time to do a little business-related schmoozing (also not the most wholesome thing for children to witness, especially if they're *your* children and you happen to be kissing someone's business butt). Those who have their own children will relish the chance to be among adults for a couple of precious hours; and for those who do not have them, even if they adore them, this is not the time they want to be cooing over a friend's precious little one.

If it's your own kids in question, spring for a baby-sitter—one who will sit for them *outside* of your home. You can even share the sitter with a couple of your guests who also have kids—at *their* home (unless you have an enormous home). If you don't make the mistake that my parents made, cloistering us kids at one end of the house while all the fun went on, ice clinking in glasses, etc., on the other side of the house, your children won't glamorize the image of cocktail parties, and they won't be driven to doing anything as silly as writing entire books singing cocktail parties' praises when they grow up.

M E N U   P L A N N I N G

LIGHTING FOR A GARDEN COCKTAIL PARTY

Now it's time to start thinking about what to serve in terms of cocktails and finger food. Assuming you've decided on the Quintessential or "Swell" Cocktail Party rather than a theme party, you'll have some decisions to make.

To start with, think about the weather. Will it be a warm-weather party or a cool- or cold-weather party? To some extent, this will determine the type of hors d'oeuvres and drinks you'll select. If it's summertime and you have an attractive backyard, you may want to have your party outside. City apartment dwellers who have a terrace may want to leave the door open, and have the party spill out onto the terrace. Or make it a roof or garden cocktail party.

In the winter, a fire in the hearth might provide a cozy backdrop for your cocktail party.

COCKTAILS

Okay. We've pussyfooted around long enough—it's time to get down to business. What's a cocktail party without cocktails? You got it! It's not a cocktail party. Therefore, at this point, you should decide what type of cocktails you'll be offering. Unless you happen to be wealthy enough to hire a bartender and have a fully stocked bar, it's a good idea to limit the choices to two or three house cocktails and two or three nonalcoholic drinks.

Choose something "brown," something "white," and something special.

"Brown" drinks are anything made with whiskey—Scotch, bourbon, rye, Canadian—or cognac. Here are the most classic of the "brown" cocktails:

MANHATTAN

ROB ROY

OLD-FASHIONED

SIDECAR

WHISKEY SOUR

"White" drinks are anything made with gin, vodka, or rum. The most classic, not only of the "white" cocktails, but really of *any* cocktail, is the martini. And by the way, "mar-

COCKTAILS AROUND THE WORLD

ENGLISH	COCKTAIL
TURKISH	KOKTEYL
PORTUGUESE	COQUETEL
KOREAN	KAKTEL
RUSSIAN	KAKTYAYL
SPANISH	COCTEL
CATALAN	COCTÉL
GERMAN	COCKTAIL
DUTCH	COCKTAIL
FRENCH	COCKTAIL
ITALIAN	MISCUGLIO DI LIQUORI

DO NOT OVERSTAY YOUR WELCOME.

☾

tini" means "gin martini." While vodka martinis are more popular nationwide than regular martinis, which are made with gin, one still has to say "vodka martini," which to me is a big clue that they're a variation on a theme. Anyway, the extra-dry gin martini, practically nothing but good quality gin with a whisper of dry vermouth, garnished with an olive, is the classic. It's cool, clean, refreshing, and serious and amusing at the same time. That's why I not only list it first here, but encourage you to include it in your cocktail party. On the other hand, in the historical progression toward the driest of dry martinis possible, another wonderful cocktail has gotten lost: the traditional martini—three parts gin, one part dry vermouth. Perhaps it's time for a comeback. Classic "white" cocktails:

MARTINI

TRADITIONAL MARTINI

VODKA MARTINI

GIN GIMLET

DAIQUIRI

SCREWDRIVER

GIN & TONIC

VODKA & TONIC

BLOODY MARY

BRONX COCKTAIL

In choosing a third cocktail, try to pick something classic, with a little panache, but not over-the-top weird. Here are a few of my favorite classic specialty cocktails:

NEGRONI

CHAMPAGNE COCKTAIL

CUBA LIBRE

PEACH BELLINI

PLANTER'S PUNCH

MINT JULEP

COGNAC MARTINI

When choosing your house cocktails, try to ensure there will be something for everyone. To do that, choose two or three that are different enough—in other words, you wouldn't want to choose a Watermelon Martini, a Piña Colada, and a Peach Bellini, because they're all fruity. You wouldn't want a Manhattan along with an Old-Fashioned, because they're both whiskey drinks that are a little sweet.

Here, then, are a few enchanting combinations:

OLD-FASHIONED, MARTINI, AND CHAMPAGNE COCKTAIL

ROB ROY, GIN GIMLET, AND PLANTER'S PUNCH

MANHATTAN AND KIR ROYALE

TURKEY SHOOT, VODKA MARTINI, AND NEGRONI

WATERMELON MARTINI AND MINT JULEP

You get the idea. Another choice is to serve only one of the above, white wine, and something nonalcoholic. But for heaven's sake, don't serve a lousy white wine, and especially don't serve a white Zinfandel, which is cloyingly sweet. Instead, try a good California Chardonnay or Sauvignon Blanc, or just about any French white table wine (George Deboeuf

GIN & TONIC

imports a very drinkable one at less than five dollars a bottle), or, if you can afford it, a French Chablis.

But once you've decided on your house cocktails, there are a few details you'll need to attend to. And I've always felt that brown drinks—Scotch, bourbon, rye, and cognac-based cocktails—are best in cool weather, even on the rocks. In any case, if it's hot out, you'll gravitate toward more summery drinks—martinis, gin & tonics, vodka drinks, and rum drinks. (Summer is when the alcohol-free drinks really sparkle, but more on that in a moment.)

Also, unless you're serving a champagne drink, have on hand at least a magnum (a double bottle) each of red and white wine—if you don't know what to look for and don't live in California, choose an inexpensive French table wine and you can't go too wrong. . . .

Next think about the mixers and supplementary liquors you'll need. For instance, if you're serving gimlets, martinis, and Manhattans, you'll need lime juice for the gimlets, dry vermouth for the martinis, sweet vermouth and bitters for the Manhattans, as well as the gin and bourbon.

If you're tempted to include beer, resist, heeding—

RULE #3: NO BEER.

Now start a list of the liquors and mixers you'll need for the cocktails you've selected, using the recipes in Chapter 6 as a guide.

How do you know how much liquor to buy? Figure on about three drinks per person. The average cocktail calls for

1½ ounces of spirits, so there are 16–17 drinks in a fifth, or 50 to every three bottles. Most liquor stores will accept returns on unopened bottles—check with yours before you purchase. In any case, it's better to have too much than too little, unless you know a liquor store that will deliver pronto. For champagne drinks, allow half a bottle per person, just in case every single person decides to have them (which, believe it or not, *is* in the realm of possibility—little drink crazes can get started even within the bounds of a single cocktail party). You may have lots of bubbly left over, but if you do, I hope that's the *worst* thing that ever happens to you.

And what about garnishes? This important question brings us to—

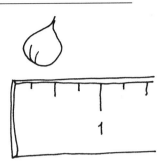

COCKTAIL ONION

RULE #4: A LEMON IS NOT A LIME.

Gin & tonics get limes. Manhattans get maraschino cherries. Martinis get olives or lemon twists. Gibsons get cocktail onions. Lillet gets a slice of orange. And so forth. *If you forget everything else you read, remember this:* **The garnish makes the cocktail, and the cocktail makes the party.** Turn to Chapter 6 and look up the drinks you've decided on for your first party. Figure out what garnishes you'll need, and add them to your shopping list.

ORANGE SLICE

LIME SQUEEZE

A L C H O H O L - F R E E   Z O N E

SHIRLEY TEMPLE

You never know who's twelve-stepping these days, and many recovering alcoholics who are comfortable enough to attend parties where there is alcohol may not appreciate it being shoved in their faces. Not only that, but many people will have one cocktail, and then switch to something nonalcoholic; or there may be designated drivers among your guests, which I heartily recommend.

But don't *penalize* these people for their abstention; your job as host is to make the cocktail party enchanting for *all* your guests. Therefore, provide two or three alcohol-free drinks that will be as intriguing to those of your guests who are partaking as they will be to those who are abstaining. Colder weather lends itself nicely to alcohol-free *classics,* such as the Shirley Temple, which is also not bad at inducing a Proustian swoon in those of us who were treated to Shirley Temples as kids (something about the combination of the maraschino cherry and the grenadine . . .), or a fresh, spicy Virgin Mary, with an irresistible zing of freshly grated horseradish. In spring or summer, who could refuse a Lemon Twist, an Orange Flower, or a Blue Tahiti? Recipes for alcohol-free drinks follow in Chapter 6, along with a number of appealing low-alcohol potations, but you should also have on hand an additional one liter of soda water for every three or four guests (depending on your crowd)—and I suggest something more *soigné* than seltzer. My friend Charles invented something called a Water Cocktail, where he mixed in precise proportions two of his favorite bottled sparkling waters and tap water. Or you might try a Classic Water Cocktail: drop a sugar cube in the bottom of a martini glass, sprinkle with bitters, fill with sparkling water, and garnish with a healthy squeeze of lemon and a maraschino cherry. (*Note:* The Classic Water Cocktail is not *completely* alcohol-free—even though you use only a few drops of bitters, they do contain 45 percent alcohol. . . .)

Tonic water is also handy, not only as a mixer, but as a drink, especially in the summer. Try the Virgin Gin & Tonic or the Virgin Vodka & Tonic (recipes in Chapter 6, but you can probably imagine . . .).

And just because a drink doesn't contain alcohol, don't skimp on the garnishes! The point is, we don't want to make our guests who don't drink alcohol feel like second-class citizens just because they happen to be at a cocktail party.

F I N G E R   F O O D

Again, start with the weather. If it's cold out, you'll want to concentrate on warm and room-temperature hors d'oeuvres. If it's summer and you have a backyard, you may want to take advantage of the several hors d'oeuvre recipes in Chapter 5 that may be prepared on the grill. And we've all noticed how cold weather puts one in the mood for richer, more substantial food, and summer makes us want to keep it light and fresh.

In either case, with your canapés and hors d'oeuvres, the effect we're going for is *soigné*. This means not big and not sloppy. Which reminds me:

RULE #5: IF YOU NEED A FORK TO EAT IT, FORGET ABOUT IT.

Finger food is finger food—beautiful, tasty little morsels to delight the eye and the palate, and above all, impress your guests. And it's amazingly easy to impress people with canapés and the like, just by doing things such as putting little sprigs of chervil or fennel on every piece of shrimp. But however they're garnished, your guests should be able to eat them in one bite—or two, if the guest is an extra-dainty type. Anything bigger requires a plate, and once you introduce plates, your cocktail party starts looking suspiciously like a dinner party in disguise.

SOIGNÉ FINGER FOOD

Finger food falls into three categories: hot hors d'oeuvres, cold hors d'oeuvres, and canapés—but all three fall under the general term hors d'oeuvre. If you have trouble pronouncing French, you can say "OR-*DER*-VIE," or in the plural "OR-*DER*-VEEZ." It isn't at all correct, but anyone who knows will understand that you're just being cute.

The ideal cocktail party, which of course yours will be, offers selections from each category. If you're having a theme party of some sort, select finger foods from Chapter 5 that go with your theme; finger foods appropriate to the Quintessential Cocktail Party also appear in abundance.

The number of types of hors d'oeuvres you'll want to

serve depends on the number of guests you expect. See the sidebar to figure how many to select.

The number of hors d'oeuvres each guest will *eat* is in some ways simpler, and in some ways more complicated. Many restaurants that cater cocktail parties figure on six per person. But there's never really enough and the greedier (or hungrier) types position themselves cleverly next to the kitchen so they can sample everything as it comes out and not be overlooked by whoever is passing them. Through my own careful research and calculations I have determined that eight to ten per person is the correct number. But this depends on many things. Firstly, it assumes that you use the recipes included herein, which make small hors d'oeuvres. If your guests think they're going to try to make a meal out of your hors d'oeuvres, you may be caught short. Again, it's up to you to let them know they'll have to proceed along to dinner afterward. Also, lighter hors d'oeuvres will go faster than heavier ones (so allow more of them) and the weather may affect your guests' appetites as well.

NUMBER OF GUESTS	TYPES OF HORS D'OEUVRES
12–16	3–4
16–24	4–5
24+	5–6

☾

A LITTLE MATTER OF CRUDITÉS AND DIPS

Certain food writers have propounded of late that guests are happy to put things together themselves, so that one should just leave out big bowls of dip and crudités and little squares of bread and cheese and such and let the guests go to work.

BAR SPOON

COCKTAIL SHAKER

MARTINI PITCHER

This is preposterous. The whole *point* of a cocktail party is that guests get to eat beautiful little hors d'oeuvres and canapés, that the gracious host does all the work beforehand, and then all the guests have to do is enjoy themselves. The proof is in the fact that if you attend a cocktail party where there are platters of hors d'oeuvres and canapés and a big thing of crudités, the crudités are *always* eaten last! This fact is irrefutable. While I personally adore crudités, I strongly feel they are best left to gatherings of family and close friends, barbecues, sporting events on TV—parties of a more casual—nay, *haphazard*—nature.

That said (and I do feel much better having gotten it off my chest), in the following chapter you'll find an indispensable collection of recipes for swell and *soigné* cocktail party finger food—more than you'll ever need, though surely once you sample a few, you'll want to try them all.

Choose the appropriate number of kinds of hors d'oeuvres, figure out exactly how many of each you'll need, and multiply the recipes accordingly. Then, using the lists of ingredients, add everything you'll need to your shopping list. The recipe will also note any special kitchen equipment you'll need for preparation.

SERVING STUFF

The magic word is: doilies. It's incredible what a mere doily can do. First of all, they're easy to find—either at the supermarket, party shop, restaurant supply store, or even the stationery and card shop. The reason they're so important is that if garnishes are king, serving trays are queen. What you do is pick up some large round serving trays—I found some very inexpensive glass ones at Woolworth's (and surely you can find them at a restaurant supply store), or you can even use aluminum pizza trays. With large doilies on them, they look spiff! The point is simply that you need to have them—probably three or four of them. Avoid regular old dinner plates—usually their flat surface isn't very big, and all the hors d'oeuvres will slide into the middle, embarrassing you to no end and ruining an otherwise perfect cocktail party.

As we know, you won't be needing plates or flatware, but you'll have to buy some attractive or amusing cocktail napkins to have handy at the bar, as well as to serve with the finger food. If you really want to be dapper, try to find some cloth cocktail napkins. In any case, if you're a flea market, antique store, or tag sale type, vintage cloth cocktail napkins are not too hard to find, and may supply a charmingly whimsical touch.

As for barware, you'll need the following: an ice bucket and tongs, a cocktail shaker, a martini pitcher and stirring rod or long bar spoon, a corkscrew, and a jigger. You'll also need a cocktail strainer if your pitcher doesn't have a little lip to catch the ice.

To serve the drinks, plastic cups are *okay,* sort of, but only if you don't really want to do it right. Part of the problem is with plastic you sacrifice an important aural element: the sound of the ice clinking in the glasses. Therefore, use them only if for some reason it means you cannot have the

JIGGER

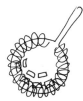

COCKTAIL STRAINER

OLD-FASHIONED GLASS

STEMMED COCKTAIL (MARTINI)

GLASS

CHAMPAGNE FLUTE

DURALEX BISTRO GLASS

party otherwise. If you do use plastic, use the short kind, in clear plastic. These are suitable for wine and sparkling water as well as cocktails. If you're serving champagne or champagne cocktails, you can pick up some plastic champagne flutes—they're pretty swell, for plastic, though there are real glass ones available for just a few cents more per glass.

If you're using glass, as I hope you are, you'll need plenty of 6-ounce old-fashioned glasses—this is what you'll use for on-the-rocks drinks—and 3-ounce stemmed cocktail glasses or martini glasses. You may need tumblers (for tall drinks), wineglasses, champagne flutes, or sherry glasses. Consult Chapter 6, which not only lists drinks along with their garnishes, but the appropriate glass as well.

If you plan on having more than one cocktail party in your lifetime (and surely you'll enjoy the first one so much you'll have dozens more . . .) it might be worth it to make the small investment required to have enough glasses for twenty-four or so guests. The Duralex bistro-type glasses imported from France can be picked up very cheaply—and the 6-ounce old-fashioned size is quite useful. Or perhaps you might try a restaurant supply store.

Alternatively, you can rent glasses, and even serving pieces you might need for your cocktail party. That way, you just make a phone call, and the rental company (check your yellow pages under Rental Services) will probably even deliver your glassware to your home, for a surprisingly low cost.

Add any serving trays, doilies, and barware you'll need to your, by now, rather extensive shopping list.

M U S I C

The last thing you'll have to consider is music, which brings us to

RULE #6: NO ONE BUT YOU TOUCHES THE STEREO.

In the best of all possible cocktail party worlds, your stereo is in the other room, and only the speakers are in the party room.

If you have a CD changer, you're in cocktail party music heaven. You can put in six CDs with suitable cocktail party music, and have the changer or carousel randomly select tracks for the perfect cocktail party ambiance. If you've been putting off buying a CD player, really I think you've waited long enough—they're remarkably affordable now. And the CD changer–type costs only slightly more than a regular one-CD player.

If, however, you choose to continue to resist CDs, you can easily make do with cassettes. Make two ninety-minute party tapes, with a variety of stunningly atmospheric selections.

In either case, you should hide or lock up all your other tapes and CDs, so you can maintain complete control over your party mood.

In general, instrumental music is preferred over vocal music (with a few exceptions). In fact, there is a whole genre of music called "cocktail piano"—and it is from this tradition that many of our finest jazz pianists hearken, both living and

69

departed. Therefore, look for recordings of solo piano by the greats—and this, too, may provide a charming and unintimidating introduction to jazz for your uninitiated guests.

Here's my personal playlist to get you started; and other specific selections for theme parties are mentioned in the previous chapter. In any case, as you browse through these, surely you'll think of a million things *you* love that you'll want to include.

The first entry on the list, *Classic Jazz Piano 1927–1957,* is an anthology that not only contains classics played by Duke Ellington, Billy Strayhorn, Count Basie, Errol Garner, and other greats, it also happens to begin in the year 1927—which is my best guess as to the birth of the cocktail party, and goes through 1957—the height of the glory days of the cocktail party.

COCKTAIL PARTY
PLAYLIST

SOLO PIANO

CLASSIC JAZZ PIANO 1927–1957 (BLUEBIRD)

JAKI BYARD AT MAYBECK (MAYBECK RECITAL HALL SERIES VOL. 17, CONCORD JAZZ)

THE PIANO STYLE OF NAT KING COLE (CAPITOL JAZZ)

BILL EVANS, SOLO SESSIONS VOLUMES I AND II (MILESTONE)

EARL HINES, MASTERS OF JAZZ, VOL. II

THELONIOUS MONK ALONE IN SAN FRANCISCO (RIVERSIDE)

THELONIOUS MONK, <u>LONDON COLLECTION, VOL. I</u> (BLACK LION)

BUD POWELL, <u>THE GENIUS OF BUD POWELL</u> (VERVE)

<u>THE ART TATUM SOLO MASTERPIECES, VOLS. 1—4</u> (PABLO)

MCCOY TYNER, <u>SOLILOQUY</u> (BLUE NOTE)

FATS WALLER, <u>PIANO MASTERWORKS VOL. 1 1922—29</u> (EPM)

JAZZ CLASSICS

MILES DAVIS, <u>KIND OF BLUE</u>

THE DAVE BRUBECK QUARTET, <u>TIME OUT</u> (FEATURING "TAKE FIVE")

JOHN COLTRANE, <u>THE GENTLER SIDE OF JOHN COLTRANE</u>

COUNT BASIE, <u>KANSAS CITY 7</u>

CANNONBALL ADDERLY, <u>SOMETHING ELSE</u>

LOUIS ARMSTRONG AND DUKE ELLINGTON, <u>THE COMPLETE LOUIS ARMSTRONG AND DUKE ELLINGTON SESSIONS</u>

BILL EVANS, <u>YOU MUST BELIEVE IN SPRING</u>

STAN GETZ, <u>THE GIRL FROM IPANEMA, THE BOSSA NOVA YEARS</u>

STAN GETZ, <u>FOCUS</u>

STAN GETZ, <u>ANNIVERSARY</u>

CHET BAKER, <u>THE BEST OF CHET BAKER PLAYS</u>

<u>ERROL GARNER PLAYS GERSHWIN AND KERN</u>

DAVE GRUSIN, <u>HOMAGE TO DUKE</u>

VOCALS AND MISCELLANEOUS

<u>JOHN COLTRANE AND JOHNNY HARTMAN</u>

<u>IT COULD HAPPEN TO YOU: CHET BAKER SINGS</u>

<u>LET'S GET LOST: THE BEST OF CHET BAKER SINGS</u>

BILLIE HOLIDAY, <u>THE FIRST VERVE SESSIONS</u>

71

ELLA FITZGERALD AND LOUIS ARMSTRONG, <u>ELLA AND LOUIS</u>

ELLA FITZGERALD, <u>FIRST LADY OF SONG</u>

ELLA FITZGERALD, <u>COLE PORTER SONGBOOK</u>

LOUIS PRIMA AND KEELY SMITH, <u>THE WILDEST</u>

HERB ALPERT, <u>MIDNIGHT SUN</u>

<u>HERB ALPERT AND THE TIJUANA BRASS</u>

FRANK SINATRA AND COUNT BASIE, <u>SINATRA AND BASIE</u>

FRANK SINATRA, <u>SONGS FOR SWINGIN' LOVERS</u>

By now much has been accomplished, and it's time to make the following final decisions:

- Date
- Time
- Guest list
- Quintessential or "Swell" Cocktail Party or theme party
- Cocktails
- Alcohol-free drinks
- Hors d'oeuvres
- Music

You're on your way! Now wait until two weeks before the party, then start telephoning or mailing the invitations. Find your finger food and drink recipes from Chapters 5 and 6, complete your shopping lists, and proceed to Chapter 4, Putting Everything Together.

4

PUTTING EVERYTHING
TOGETHER

Okay. It's ten days before the party, you've invited the guests, and the last RSVPs are starting to come in. Aren't you pleased at the positive response? This week, and into next, we'll attend to some annoying yet important details, such as deciding how to arrange furniture and lighting in your party room, creating an ambiance with decor, making music tapes if you so choose, and finally doing your preliminary shopping.

ARRANGING FURNITURE

The furniture question brings us directly to

RULE #7: "NO SITTING."

"NO SITTING!"

You'll have to plan on removing all chairs, loveseats, divans, and chaise longues. (If you can't move your sofa, you'll have to find some large, pointy objects—replicas of the Eiffel Tower or the Empire State Building, band saws, or small appliances—to store on it to discourage sitting.) The no-sitting rule has been codified into cocktail party law precisely because it is so very important. As author Margaret Visser explains in her book *The Rituals of Dinner*, standing room in a cocktail party allows for "production of chance encounters; sufficient room is provided so that guests can both approach and escape from one another."

A happy result turns out to be that once all the chairs are stashed away, your room becomes larger than you think. Nevertheless, don't invite so many people that your room is overcrowded: guests who are jammed, sardine-style, shoulder to shoulder, can't easily escape from a bore (or a boor) by using the old "I'm ready for another drink, may I get you one?" excuse. (More on this useful tactic in Chapter 7.)

Those fortunate enough to live in a house or apartment with a wet bar (a big fad for homes built in the fifties and sixties) should take advantage and set up the bar there. For those of us not so lucky (meaning most of us), there are several other options. If you have an open kitchen that spills out into the living room, it may be best to set up the bar on a convenient kitchen counter, but not if it takes up too much valuable counterspace, which you'll need for last-minute hors d'oeuvre preparation. If you have a pass-through counter from your kitchen to the party room, this works quite nicely; otherwise move a table into the living room, and cover it with an attractive cloth (white damask or vintage linen is nicest for a Quintessential Cocktail Party). And if you're opting for a theme party, select a tablecloth accordingly. For instance, for a Third World Party, haul out an Indian bedspread! Or for a South-of-the-Border Party, a serape would be most fetching. Bali Hai Party? What's wrong with a sarong? Use that old one you never knew how to tie up properly anyway.

So this will be your bar, and it must be large enough to hold glasses, ice bucket, cocktail shaker or pitcher, bowls of garnishes, and whatever bottles of liquor, mixers, and alcohol-free drinks you'll need.

You'll also want to have a place where you can put trays of hors d'oeuvres after they have been passed once (unless of course you have help or you plan to hire wait-staff to tend bar or pass hors d'oeuvres). This may be a dining table—pushed against the wall if space is a problem—or an accessible counter. Coffee tables don't do the trick—they're too low, so you're probably best off moving them out of the party space.

End tables *are* useful, however, since they're a little higher; strategically placed, they're ideal for guests to rest their drinks on. Cover them with small cloths (oversized cloth napkins may be the perfect size), or scatter coasters on them.

And if you don't mind smoking in your home, do yourself a big favor and supply *plenty* of ashtrays—many more than you think necessary unless you're very fond of cleaning up cigarette butts. Figure on at least one per end table, and

DO NOT BRING FLOWERS. IF YOU MUST BRING A GIFT, BRING SOMETHING THAT DOES NOT HAVE TO BE ATTENDED TO, SUCH AS WINE OR CHOCOLATES.

☾

many more throughout. If you have houseplants, try leaving an ashtray in the soil of each one to outwit those who would snub out their ciggies in them.

DECOR

Unless you're having a theme party, you don't need to do anything special in terms of the decor. Think of it this way: your beautiful canapés and cocktail garnishes will *become* your decor. What makes most sense here is simply to consider a color scheme. Coordinate your cocktail napkins and table coverings—which doesn't mean they have to be the same color, only that they look well together—and think about how they will look with whatever lighting you'll be using (see below). And don't forget that the cocktail toothpicks with frilly hats which we so adore can be purchased not only in assorted colors, but also separately in either yellow, red, blue, or green.

If you have selected a theme, refer back to Chapter 1 for specific decor ideas for each particular theme cocktail party.

LIGHTING

Where lighting is concerned, there's nothing worse than a glaring overhead light, which brings us to

RULE #8: NO GLARING OVERHEAD LIGHTS.

Instead, lighting should be soft and arranged at a flattering height. A cocktail party shouldn't be too dark, however, lest the charming symbolic significance of the cocktail hour as passage from day into evening be lost. And of course your lighting concerns will be different if it is the end of June and your cocktail party will be held in Anchorage, Alaska, than they will be if it's the middle of December and you're in Boston.

In spring and summer, one amusing option is to string up Japanese lanterns overhead—a height of about six and a half feet should be right unless you know a lot of basketball players. Strung across the room at intervals of five feet or so, the lanterns will lend even the drabbest party room instant pizzazz. Or if pizzazz isn't your cup of tea and you're more the panache type, look for strings of carnival sockets (available at lighting stores, some hardware stores, and sometimes party rental companies), which are what are used at Italian street fairs and the like. You can use small round white bulbs in them for a soigné effect. In fact, you can even use the strings of small white Christmas lights that languish in the bottom of a closet all year. Multicolored Christmas bulbs give an entirely more funky effect, and the strings of lights shaped like chili peppers, fruit, fish, etc., that have become popular in recent years are a festive option as well. (Of course you'll consider your theme if you're going the festive route. I've seen strings of skulls that would be perfect for a Mexican Day of the Dead cocktail party.)

VOTIVE CANDLE

Wall sconces are terrific if you happen to have them (very Nick and Nora Charles), for they offer a gentle luminescence at an ideal height. But don't fret if you don't have them, for one of the most attractive options is most easily achievable by anyone in any kind of party room: Place votive candles in little glasses all over the place, at different heights. You can find them in a Pottery Barn or Crate & Barrel type store, or even a hardware store, party store, or grocery store. White votives in clear or frosted white glasses are the most elegant; a single color of votives (green, for instance) in clear or frosted white can be quite striking; and assorted colors of glasses—red, blue, yellow, green—with white votives lend a funky-retro feeling. Strings of white Christmas lights go with anything, as do votive candles. Japanese lanterns go with Retro Party or Blue Hawaii, etc.

COATROOM

One other tiny little detail that should be attended to ahead of time is what to do with people's wraps. Of course this won't be a problem in warm weather, but people may still have bags and things. Usually it will be sufficient to designate a bedroom as the coatroom, and lay all the coats on the bed. However, if you are expecting a large crowd and you are renting glasses or other bar equipment, you might consider renting a coat rack from the party rental company as well. That way guests can easily find their wraps without having to dig through an entire mountain of coats. In any case, the important thing to know is *where* you would like guests to leave their coats so you don't have an unplanned glitch just as the cocktail party is beginning.

S H O P P I N G   A H E A D

There are plenty of tasks you can get out of the way well ahead of time—say a week before the party—including a lot of the shopping. I highly recommend this, because you want to have as few things to do as possible just before.

A week before the party, look at your shopping list, and pick up:

- All your barware (order well beforehand if you're renting, especially if it's party season)
- Serving trays
- Doilies
- Tablecloths, if you don't have appropriate ones
- Anything you need for lighting
- CDs and blank cassette tapes, if necessary
- Ashtrays, if you're allowing smoking and you don't have a lot of them
- Frilly toothpicks, extra-long cocktail toothpicks, and the like
- Any kitchen equipment you need to make your recipes (though this is not usually necessary)
- All your liquor
- All your mixers

- Any nonperishables on your shopping list, such as flour, anchovies, Worcestershire sauce, maraschino cherries, olives, etc.

DO-AHEAD PREPARATION

TWO TO SEVEN DAYS BEFORE

A week before the party, make sure any tablecloths you'll be using are laundered and ironed, and any rentals have been ordered. If you're making party tapes, you should give yourself at least a week. Recording songs from a CD player to a cassette tape is much less time consuming than it used to be with a turntable, but it still requires a certain vigilance, and you only have the length of each song to do something else in-between. In any case, two ninety-minute tapes will more than cover the duration of your cocktail party.

Two or three days—even up to a week—before the party, you can do a lot of the preparation for hors d'oeuvres. Read through the recipes and see if there are things that may be prepared in advance, such as pastry shells, Cheese Straws, gravlax, the filling for Endives with Gorgonzola and Walnut, or rosemary oil for Grilled Rosemary Shrimp. If you want to make any hot hors d'oeuvres ahead and freeze them, now's the time to do that, too. Also prepare spiced nuts up to four or five days before.

THE DAY BEFORE

The day before the party, do the rest of your shopping. If you're making something that needs to be chilled, such as shrimp, the day before is the earliest you'd want to do it—if you do it before, it won't be fresh enough; if you buy it the morning of the party, it won't be chilled enough unless you can cook it in the morning. Get a jump on tomorrow by preparing any sauces or fillings that won't be hurt by a day of refrigeration, such as sauce for the Stilton and Port Canapés, the vinaigrette for Firecracker Endives, or any of the smoked fish mousse fillings. Anything that needs overnight marination, such as ceviche for stuffing into tomatoes, or chicken for Tiki, Jerk, or Barbecue Drumettes, should be attended to as well.

If feasible (and depending on whether you have a lot to do the day of), you can also arrange your furniture and stereo the way you want it (keeping handy the CDs you've selected or the tapes you've made), and arrange the lighting.

Finally, set up the bar, including the ice bucket (empty at this point, of course!) and tongs, long bar spoon or cocktail stirring rod, cocktail strainer, martini pitcher, cocktail shaker, jigger, bottles of spirits, and bitters, Worcestershire sauce, and any other accoutrements you might require. (If you do this the night before, you'll be sure to know way ahead of time if you're missing something!) Neatly lay out the glassware, make a stack of cocktail napkins, and put mixers, mineral water, juice, white wine, champagne, etc., in the refrigerator to chill.

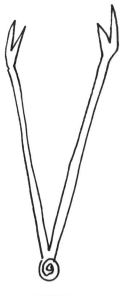

ICE TONGS

Now relax, breathe through your nose, and rejoice in the fact that you're two-thirds of the way there!

DON'T BE SAD IF YOU DON'T HAVE LINEN COCKTAIL NAPKINS—IF YOU'RE USING PAPER, YOU CAN MAKE A PROFESSIONAL-LOOKING COCKTAIL NAPKIN SPIRAL EASILY AT HOME. SIMPLY PUT THEM IN A NEAT STACK ABOUT FIVE TO EIGHT INCHES IN HEIGHT, PRESS DOWN HARD ON TOP WITH A STURDY TUMBLER OR BOTTLE, AND TWIST! TURN PILE OVER AND REPEAT TO COMPLETE THE TWIST. THE FINAL PRODUCT WILL LOOK LIKE ONE OF THOSE SPIRAL NOTE-PADS.

☾

THE DAY OF THE PARTY

Much of the final work must be done the day of the party.

Morning and Early Afternoon. In the morning, put together garnishes for drinks (consulting Chapter 6), and make "easy syrup" if necessary. Set each individual garnish in a separate bowl, cover with plastic wrap, and refrigerate until just before guests arrive. (Citrus will dry out if done too early.) Elaborate cocktail garnishes, such as those for old-fashioneds, are best done assembly-line style—in other words, first cut all the orange slices, then cut the wide pieces of lemon peel, then drain the maraschino cherries, put each of the three ingredients in bowls, line them up, and assemble them. Store in a bowl covered with plastic in the refrigerator.

Next do all the prep for the finger food that couldn't be done a day or more ahead of time.

First come the garnishes. For herb garnishes, carefully select the most attractive leaves, and snip them with scissors. Place in a bowl with a dampened paper towel over them to keep them fresh, and refrigerate. Drain anything that needs it, such as capers or anchovies; refrigerate. Any other garnishes that need to be cooked in any way should be taken care of now as well.

Take out butter from the fridge if you need to soften it for canapés. If using herb butter or other flavored butters, make them once the butter is soft. Keep either plain or flavored butters just soft enough (without letting them melt) by keeping an eye on them—and of course the room temperature will have an enormous effect. If the butter's getting too soft, put it back in the fridge for a while, and take it out later.

Prepare any other spread your recipes call for—such as tapenade or flavored mayonnaise.

Cut up any vegetables you'll need as ingredients (chop onions, mince shallots, etc.).

Assemble any hors d'oeuvres that won't wilt or get soggy, such as Prosciutto and Melon with Port-Pepper Sauce, Stuffed Celery Gems, Scallop Brochettes Laced with Bacon (of course you'll leave the cooking until later), and Radishes with Anchovy Cream.

If you're using packaged bouchées, the morning is the time to crisp them in the oven.

Late Afternoon: Canapés. Canapés have to wait until last to be assembled or else they'll become soggy and unappealing.

In general, the thing to keep in mind when faced with the daunting task of assembling hundreds of hors d'oeuvres is to work like an assembly line. It's remarkable how much faster things go this way! For instance, if you're peeling and deveining shrimp, first peel all of them. Then make a shallow slice in each along the length. Then move to the sink, pull the veins out, and rinse them. This is much faster than repeating the steps for each shrimp, wasting a lot of time and energy moving back and forth.

COCKTAIL RYE, CRUST TRIMMED

When making canapés, first have all your ingredients in front of you in little bowls.

The fastest way to mass-produce canapés is to use whole, unsliced bread—a Pullman loaf (available from many good bakeries) works best. Cut the crust off one long side, then slice the loaf lengthwise into ¼-inch slices, *then* cut off the rest of the crusts. Spread *all of them* with your compound butter or spread, pipe decorative butter or spread along the edges if necessary, chill for thirty minutes, *then* cut all of them into rectangles or triangles or use cookie or biscuit cutters for round or fanciful shapes, and garnish, assembly line–style, at the end.

If you don't need enormous numbers of canapés, there are two other ways to do bread bases. The first is to use regular slices of bread, toast them lightly if necessary (especially if the bread is very soft), then cut shapes with biscuit or cookie cutters or a small sharp knife. Another option is to use the slim square loaves of cocktail pumpernickel or cocktail rye, stack them up four or five high, and cut off their crusts. These are actually a nice option because they're dense and hold together well.

Once the bread bases are the proper shape, line them up on baking sheets (which are great for storing them in the fridge), apply the flavored butter or other spread to all of them, pipe a border if desired, and chill for thirty minutes. Apply the first layer of garnish to all of them, then apply the second, if any, to all of them, and then apply the sprig of herb or other tiny final decoration to all of them at the end. Carefully place plastic over the baking sheets, and file them away in the fridge. You'll want to take them out an hour or so before the party to bring them up to room temperature, and arrange them attractively on doily-bedecked trays.

One Half Hour Before. A half hour before your guests are due, preheat the oven to finish any hot hors d'oeuvres (any that are to be reheated should wait to go in the oven until the appointed hour of arrival), and do a spot-check to make sure you haven't forgotten anything.

Fifteen Minutes Before. Fifteen minutes before, light the candles, fill the ice bucket, take the chilled mixers, white wine, mineral water, etc., out of the fridge and place on the bar, start the tape or CD player in an attempt to simulate an atmosphere of relaxation, and mix any alcoholic or alcohol-free drinks that can be mixed in batches (there aren't many of these). With any luck, you'll have five minutes to sit down and catch your breath before your guests arrive.

FINGER FOOD:
COLD AND HOT
HORS D'OEUVRES
AND CANAPÉS

In the following pages, you'll find all the recipes you'll need to make the most enticing cocktail party finger food, no matter what your level of cooking skill. The recipes are all marked with either one, two, or three stars, indicating the difficulty of preparation. Count on those marked *to be quick and easy—accessible even to those readers who get nervous slicing a banana into cereal. The designation **may mean one of two things: either the recipe is of middle-range difficulty, or it may require more preparation (even if it's not technically difficult) than the selections marked *. Those marked ***may be a little trickier still, or they may simply be more labor-intensive or time-consuming.

Even if you happen to be an expert cook, it's still best to limit yourself to one or two recipes requiring a lot of last-minute preparation, or you'll be going nuts just before the party.

In any case, do yourself a huge favor and do as much of the preparation as you can—for any of the recipes—as far in advance of the party as is convenient. The recipes will tell you whenever this is possible.

I've never been big on high-tech kitchen gadgets, but a food processor does make many of these recipes a breeze. A blender can often stand in, but alas, not for making pastry.

If you plan on making canapés with any kind of frequency, there is, however, one gadget I would highly recommend procuring—and that is a graduated set of round biscuit cutters, preferably with a crinkled edge. The one I've fallen in love with is from the August Thomsen Corp. (Glen Cove, NY 11542)—it consists of nine nested crinkled biscuit cutters from one inch to three inches, and it's ATECO no. 5207. (No. 5257, with regular edges, is also pretty bitchin'.) They're great for cutting pretty bases for canapés in any size you'd ever want, as well as stamping out pastry dough. Cookie cutters may be used as well, and come in a wide variety of shapes, but I've found they're not as sharp, and hence, they're slower going.

To make life easier, any special equipment necessary (biscuit cutters, pastry bags, and the like) is listed at the top of each recipe. If none is listed, that means nothing unusual is required.

The fastest way to assemble hors d'oeuvres and canapés in large quantities is to work assembly-line style wherever possible. When assembling Caviar Bouchées, for instance,

IN FRENCH, HORS-
D'OEUVRE MEANS
"OUTSIDE THE WORK,"
THE WORK BEING THE
MEAL.

☾

lay out all your bouchées (tiny patty shells) on a tray or baking sheet, then fill them all with crème fraîche, then place caviar on all of them, then garnish them. It goes so much more quickly than putting them together individually.

And finally, a note on ingredients.

Always use the finest, freshest ingredients the market has to offer, and don't hesitate to substitute something fresh and beautiful for something limp and dull. It's always best to shop for what's in season and locally grown.

Flour should be unbleached, and eggs and milk are always better when organically raised. When butter is required, use sweet unsalted butter; if using it for spreading on bread bases, you may find it more convenient to use the whipped unsalted butter that comes in a tub. For seasoning, use sea salt and freshly ground black pepper wherever possible. Herbs should be fresh rather than dried, unless otherwise noted.

Above all, cook with pleasure, and don't forget to taste!

COLD HORS D'OEUVRES AND CANAPÉS

• SMOKED SALMON CANAPÉS * •

For the most soigné canapés, use the finest smoked salmon available (you usually can't go wrong with Scotch smoked salmon or Norwegian). Save the extra scraps of salmon and either eat them yourself when no one's looking, or save them for a pasta dish with vodka and tomato, or scramble them with eggs and onion.

EQUIPMENT
    2½-INCH COOKIE CUTTERS IN FANCIFUL SHAPES OR 1¾-INCH
    ROUND BISCUIT CUTTERS

INGREDIENTS
*½ pound smoked salmon, sliced
    very thin*
*8 slices European-style
    pumpernickel bread*
Softened unsalted butter

1 tablespoon lemon juice
Capers for garnish
Shreds of lemon zest for garnish

PREPARATION

Spread bread with softened butter, and cut out shapes with cookie cutters or biscuit cutters. Use the cutters to cut out identical shapes from the salmon.

ASSEMBLY

Lay the salmon over the bread bases to fit exactly. Sprinkle with a few drops of lemon juice, and garnish with several capers and a few shreds of lemon zest.

MAKES 20 LARGE OR 36 SMALL CANAPÉS

VARIATION

Instead of garnishing with capers and lemon, fill a pastry bag fitted with a small round tip with crème fraîche (see sidebar, page 114), and pipe designs around the edges of the canapés. Garnish with a pretty chervil leaf or fennel leaves.

PASTRY BAG WITH SMALL ROUND TIP

• SMOKED TROUT CANAPÉS ** •

EQUIPMENT

    FOOD PROCESSOR OR BLENDER

INGREDIENTS

1 small smoked trout (about ½ pound)

1 avocado

2 tablespoons lemon juice

1 teaspoon Worcestershire sauce

½ teaspoon salt

⅛ teaspoon cayenne pepper

1 baguette (not too fat), cut in ¼-inch-thick rounds

Daikon sprouts for garnish

PREPARATION

In the bowl of a food processor or blender, combine avocado, lemon juice, Worcestershire sauce, salt, and cayenne pepper, and process until smooth. (*Note:* May be done up to 24 hours ahead of time and stored covered and refrigerated.)

Remove skin and bones from trout, and use a fork or small knife to separate the flesh into 36 bite-size pieces, letting the fish flake apart along its natural grain as much as possible. (*Note:* May be done up to 24 hours ahead of time and stored wrapped in plastic and refrigerated.)

Preheat oven to 350°F. Spread the baguette rounds on a baking sheet, and lightly toast on one side only for 5 minutes. (*Note:* May be done as early as the morning of the party and stored in an airtight container until ready to assemble.)

ASSEMBLY

Spread out the baguette rounds, soft side up, and spoon a small amount of avocado sauce on each. Place a piece of smoked trout on top, and garnish with 5 or 6 daikon sprouts.

MAKES 36 CANAPÉS.

• SHRIMP CANAPÉS ** •

EQUIPMENT

    FOOD PROCESSOR OR BLENDER

    PASTRY BAG FITTED WITH SMALL STAR TIP

INGREDIENTS

*½ pound medium shrimp
   (36–40 per pound)*

2 teaspoons salt

1 sandwich loaf (unsliced)

*1 cup (2 sticks) unsalted
   butter, softened*

1 cup watercress, loosely packed

⅓ cup chopped chives

⅓ cup chopped dill

1 lemon, half of it sliced

1 small onion, sliced

5 or 6 black peppercorns

*5 or 6 radishes, sliced paper-
   thin for garnish*

*48 small select pieces of dill for
   garnish*

PREPARATION

Peel and devein shrimp. Refrigerate.

    Bring 3 cups of water to boil with 2 teaspoons salt. Add watercress and blanch for 1 minute. Remove with a slotted spoon, blot with paper towels, and set aside. Add the onion, the sliced half of lemon, and peppercorns to the water, bring back to the boil, and add the shrimp. Cook 2 minutes. Drain, and refresh in ice water. Drain again, slice each in half, and squeeze the remaining lemon half over them.

    To make the herb butter, place butter, watercress, chives, and dill in the bowl of a food processor or blender, and process until creamy and completely blended.

Cut the crust off one long side of the sandwich loaf, and cut lengthwise into ¼-inch slices. Remove the other crusts.

Spread each slice with a thin layer of herb butter. Fill the pastry bag with butter, and pipe along each long edge of the bread, as shown in the illustration. Chill in refrigerator for 30 minutes.

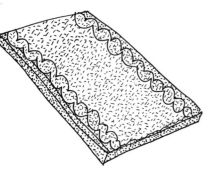

BREAD SLICED, PIPED WITH HERB BUTTER

ASSEMBLY

Cut buttered slices into 1½-inch-wide rectangles (each short end will be piped). On each slice, place 1 or 2 radish slices, 2 shrimp halves, and a tiny dill sprig on each side.

MAKES 24 CANAPÉS.

THE FINISHED CANAPÉ

• CREAM CHEESE AND OLIVE CANAPÉS * •

My mom used to make us cream cheese and olive sandwiches on Wonder Bread when I was a kid. I don't miss the Wonder Bread, but the cream cheese and olive combination not only brings back fond memories, it also happens to work perfectly for cocktail canapés.

EQUIPMENT

FOOD PROCESSOR (OPTIONAL)

FLOWER, DIAMOND, OR OTHER SHAPES OF COOKIE OR BISCUIT CUTTER, ABOUT 2½ INCHES

CREAM CHEESE AND OLIVE CANAPÉS

INGREDIENTS

1 loaf sliced pumpernickel
  bread
1 cup finely chopped green
  olives stuffed with pimentos

8 ounces cream cheese, softened
½ teaspoon Worcestershire sauce
6 radishes
2 carrots, sliced very thin

PREPARATION

Combine chopped olives, cream cheese, and Worcestershire sauce in food processor or by hand.

To prepare garnishes, make vertical cuts around each radish, then slice very thin. Cut notches out of the edges of the carrot slices to make flower shapes.

ASSEMBLY

Spread mixture on slices of pumpernickel, and cut out shapes with cookie or biscuit cutters. You should be able to get 2 or 3 from each slice of bread. Garnish each with 2 slices of radish, or a carrot flower.

MAKES 32 CANAPÉS.

• CANAPÉS NIÇOISES *** •

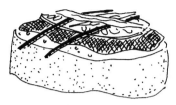

CANAPÉ NIÇOISE

This may be the most beautiful and impressive-looking of all the finger food herein; it also happens to be fabulous—each one tastes like an entire niçoise salad. And French-cutting string beans may be a pain in the neck, but did you know that on certain old-fashioned potato peelers there's a handy French-cutter for string beans? (It's the funny little square thing with two wires in it that you've been staring at all these years but never knew what it was.)

EQUIPMENT
> FOOD PROCESSOR OR BLENDER

INGREDIENTS

1 baguette
1 can tuna (6⅛-ounce size)
1 cup basil leaves
½ cup pitted niçoise or other
     black olives
Juice of ½ lemon

8 French-cut* string beans
2 hard-boiled eggs
10 cherry tomatoes, sliced
     paper-thin
16 anchovies, rinsed and cut in
     half lengthwise

PREPARATION

In a food processor or blender, combine the tuna, basil, olives, and lemon juice, and process until smooth.

Slice the baguette into ⅜-inch slices.

Separate the white from the yolks of the eggs, cut the

*Sliced vertically into very thin strips

⅛-INCH BRUNOISE

whites into *brunoise* (tiny ⅛-inch cubes—see illustration), and press the yolk through a fine sieve.

Cook the French-cut string beans in a little salted water for about 3 minutes, and plunge into ice water to stop cooking. Drain.

ASSEMBLY

Spread each baguette slice with some of the tuna-olive paste. To garnish, first sprinkle a little egg yolk over it, then top with a few tiny cubes of egg white; over that place a slice of tomato, then two pieces of string bean, and over that two pieces of anchovy, placed in an X.

MAKES ABOUT 32 CANAPÉS.

• BLACK AND WHITE CAVIAR CANAPÉS * •

These striking canapés with back-to-back triangles of caviar and egg white were designed expressly with the Black and White theme party in mind. But they'd also be delicious with the yolks added in and onions sprinkled on top.

INGREDIENTS

8 slices thin-sliced white bread*

½ cup (1 stick) softened unsalted butter

2 ounces caviar (Sevruga, Osetra, or Beluga)

3 hard-boiled eggs, whites only

PREPARATION

Force egg whites through a sieve, using the back of a spoon (this squishes them into squiggly bits). Toast bread lightly, cut off crusts, and butter. Using a sharp knife, cut toasts into 2-inch squares.

ASSEMBLY

Using a ruler to get a sharp diagonal line, place egg whites on half of the toasts, then caviar on the other half.

MAKES 32 CANAPÉS.

*Pepperidge Farm makes a good one called "Veri-Thin."

VARIATION: CAVIAR CANAPÉS

Add 1 white onion, cut into ⅛-inch brunoise, to above recipe, and use both the egg white and the yolk, put separately through the sieve. Place caviar on one side, as above; divide the other half in two, placing egg white on one half and egg yolk on the other. Scatter a few onions on top as garnish.

• CHICKEN LIVER MOUSSE CANAPÉS ** •

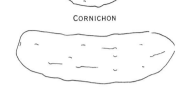

CORNICHON

DILL PICKLE (SHOWN FOR SCALE)

EQUIPMENT

> PASTRY BAG FITTED WITH LARGE STAR TIP
> FOOD PROCESSOR OR BLENDER

INGREDIENTS

1½ pounds chicken livers
¼ cup (½ stick) unsalted
*   butter*
1 onion, sliced thin
1 tablespoon cognac
1 teaspoon sugar
½ teaspoon salt
½ hard-boiled egg
½ cup heavy cream

Salt and freshly ground white
*   pepper to taste*
40 tiny tart shells (see recipe,
*   page 151), reheated and*
*   let cool if frozen*
5 cornichons, cut into brunoise*
*   (tiny ⅛-inch dice) for*
*   garnish*

PREPARATION

In a large skillet, melt the butter, add the onion, and cook over low heat until soft, about 5 minutes. Add the livers, turn up flame to medium high, and cook, stirring occasionally, for 10–12 minutes. When almost all traces of pink are gone, stir in cognac, and cook for another 4–5 minutes, or until all traces of pink are gone.

    Let the livers and onion cool, place in bowl of food

*These tiny French pickles can be found in the gourmet sections of most su-supermarkets.

processor or blender, along with sugar, salt, and hard-boiled egg, and process until smooth.

Using a whisk or electric beater, whip the cream in a medium-size bowl until it is thick, but does not yet hold peaks. Do not overwhip.

Stir the cream into the liver, adjust seasoning, and refrigerate until ready for use.

ASSEMBLY

Fill the pastry bag with mousse and, using large star tip, pipe into tiny tart shells. Garnish with a sprinkling of cornichon brunoise. Serve at once, or refrigerate up to 1 hour, covered with plastic, but not so as to disturb the mousse.

MAKES 40 CANAPÉS.

• PATÉ ROUNDS * •

INGREDIENTS

36 *juniper berries**
12 *cornichons***

1 *baguette*
½ *pound pâté, preferably a
  mousse-style pâté*

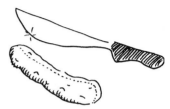

PREPARATION

Place juniper berries in a small saucepan, cover with water, bring to boil, turn down heat, and simmer for 20 minutes. Drain.

To make cornichon fans, cut each cornichon in half vertically, then make five or six parallel vertical cuts, cutting not quite all the way to the stem end, so cornichon stays together. Press down lightly in center of cornichon to spread into fan shape.

Preheat oven to 350°F. Slice baguette into 48 ¼-inch slices. Place slices on baking sheet, and bake 8–10 minutes or until very lightly toasted.

MAKING CORNICHON FANS

ASSEMBLY

Spread a small amount of pâté on each baguette slice. Garnish half with cornichon fans, and half with two or three juniper berries.

MAKES 48 CANAPÉS.

*Available in small jars in the spice department of many supermarkets.
**Found in the gourmet sections of most supermarkets.

CORNED BEEF AND CABBAGE
CANAPÉ

• CORNED BEEF AND CABBAGE CANAPÉS * •

These may sound a little weird, but they're just the thing for a St. Paddy's Day Party.

INGREDIENTS

½ head cabbage, cut in chunks and washed well
2 tablespoons malt vinegar
Salt and freshly ground white pepper to taste

½ pound corned beef, thinly sliced
1 loaf sliced cocktail pumpernickel, crusts removed
Pommery or Dijon mustard

PREPARATION

In a large saucepan, bring one inch of salted water to a boil, add the cabbage, and cook 10–15 minutes, until tender. Drain and cool, and cut into fine julienne (⅛-inch shreds). Toss with vinegar, salt, and pepper to taste.

Cut corned beef into 28 pieces, each just large enough to fit folded over on a cocktail pumpernickel square.

ASSEMBLY

Spread each pumpernickel square with mustard, lay a slice of corned beef on it, folded once, if necessary, and top with a few shreds of cabbage.

MAKES 28 CANAPÉS.

104

• GRAVLAX CANAPÉS *** •

Ever since I was a child, gravlax—Danish cured salmon—has always been one of my absolute favorite things to eat. The curing—three or four days in the refrigerator—gives the salmon a silky melt-in-your-mouth texture that's simply heavenly. It's also easily as elegant as smoked salmon at about one-sixth the cost.

The traditional recipe calls for a spruce bough along with the dill—if you happen to have one, by all means use it! Do take note that there is alcohol in this dish in the form of the Aquavit. The recipe works perfectly well without it, so feel free to omit it if you are worried about any twelve-stepping guests. If you do use the Aquavit, you may think it silly to buy a whole bottle just for three tablespoonsful. But I see it as a perfect excuse to keep the rest of the bottle in the freezer; served straight up in a tiny glass, it's an aperitif that happens to go sublimely well with Gravlax Canapés. Or try an Aurora Borealis—the smashing new cocktail that guests can't seem to refuse—it can be found in Chapter 6!

INGREDIENTS

For the gravlax:

One 2½–3 pound salmon, bones removed, but skin left on
¼ cup sea salt
¼ cup sugar

2 tablespoons crushed (not ground) black peppercorns
3 tablespoons Aquavit
1 large bunch dill

For the sauce:

⅓ cup Dijon mustard
3 tablespoons honey
¾ cup sour cream
½ bunch dill, finely chopped
    (about ¼ cup)

Salt and freshly ground white
    pepper to taste

For the assembly:

2 small square loaves sliced
    dense "European-style"
    bread, whole grain or
    pumpernickel

Juniper berries,* simmered in
    water for 15 minutes, for
    garnish
Dill sprigs for garnish

PREPARATION

For the gravlax: Run your finger along the exposed sides of
the fish, and use tweezers to pull out any small bones you
find. Place one-half of the fish skin–side down in a baking
dish. Combine salt, sugar, and pepper, and rub half of it on
the fish. Lay the dill over it to cover, and pour on the Aquavit. Rub the rest of the salt mixture into the other half of
fish, and place it, skin side up, on the first. Cover with plastic wrap, place a cutting board on top, and weight it down
with the heaviest objects you can find. I use my marble mortar and pestle, my granite *molcajete* (a Mexican guacamole ves-
sel), and a couple of marble peaches. But cans out of the
pantry do just as nicely. Refrigerate.

After 12 hours, flip the fish over, separate the filets and
spoon in some of the accumulated juices, replace the fish, and

*Available in small jars in the spice department of many supermarkets.

spoon some more over the top of the fish. Replace the plastic wrap, cutting board, and weights. Repeat this ritual every 12 hours, and cure this way for at least 3, and up to 4 days.

When the fish has cured, remove the dill, and with a very sharp knife, slice very thinly on the diagonal. (This should be done the morning of the party or the evening before.)

For the sauce: In a mixing bowl, whisk together the mustard and honey, then stir in the sour cream and dill, and salt and pepper to taste. Let sit refrigerated at least overnight, or up to 24 hours before serving, to give the flavors a chance to emerge.

ASSEMBLY

Stamp circles out of the dense bread with a 1¾-inch fluted biscuit cutter. Spoon a small amount (about ½ teaspoon) of dill sauce on each round, and top with a slice of gravlax, folded to fit the round if necessary. Garnish with a tiny sprig of dill and a juniper berry.

MAKES ABOUT 100 CANAPÉS.

CREAMED HERRING AND BEET
CANAPÉ

• CREAMED HERRING AND BEET CANAPÉS ** •

EQUIPMENT
2-INCH ROUND COOKIE OR BISCUIT CUTTER

INGREDIENTS

2 beets
⅓ cup balsamic vinegar
1 bunch parsley
2 herrings in sour cream, about ¾ pound, available at deli counter (or, if unavailable, ¾ pound of pickled herring, marinated overnight in the refrigerator in 16 ounces of sour cream)

1 white onion
1 loaf pumpernickel bread, sliced
1 tub of softened, unsalted butter for spreading on the bread
Salt and freshly ground black pepper to taste

PREPARATION (OVERNIGHT)

The night before the party: Wrap the beets, without peeling them, in aluminum foil, place them on a cookie sheet or small roasting pan, and roast them in a preheated 375°F oven for about 1 hour, or until tender when pierced with a fork. Unwrap them, and when they are cool enough, remove their skins, which should come off easily with your fingers. To julienne the beets, slice each one into thin (⅛-inch) slices, then

108

stack up the slices, and cut them into ⅛-inch strips. Put the julienned beets in a small bowl, sprinkle with salt and a few generous grinds of fresh black pepper, and cover them with the balsamic vinegar. Let marinate overnight in the refrigerator.

If using plain pickled herring, put the herrings in a bowl, add the sour cream, stir to combine, and let them marinate overnight in the refrigerator as well.

Day of the party: Finely chop the parsley; set aside in a bowl. Cut the onion into ⅛-inch brunoise (see illustration page 112)—or chop very finely; set aside in a bowl. Cut each herring crosswise into ¼-inch slices; replace in their marinade.

ASSEMBLY

Butter one side of each slice of bread. Spread the parsley on a dinner plate or cutting board, and press each slice of bread, buttered side down, into the parsley, evenly coating each. Then stamp out 2-inch circles from the slices, using the biscuit or cookie cutter. You should get 2 or 3 circles out of each slice.

On each pumpernickel round, place one piece of herring, curling it around to fit on the round, and spoon a small amount of sour cream on top. Place 2 or 3 juliennes of beet on top, and sprinkle on a little of the onion.

MAKES ABOUT 36 CANAPÉS.

• BOUCHEÉS ** •

PUFF PASTRY BOUCHÉE

Bouchées provide the most elegant of housings for a variety of fillings—from crème fraîche and caviar to smoked trout mousse to pâté de foie gras. Most people I know are afraid of making puff pastry from scratch, and in truth the frozen puff pastries available in supermarkets are pretty good. There are even some excellent commercially made bouchées that are sealed in plastic, and come in a box like crackers (find them on the shelf in gourmet and fancy food shops).

If you've always been meaning to try making puff pastry from scratch, it's actually not very difficult technically; it just takes all day. In Volume II of *Mastering the Art of French Cooking,* Julia Child and Simone Beck offer a shortcut—*Pâté Demi-Feuilletée* (which they translate as "Simple Puff Pastry" or "Mock Puff Pastry") that takes less than four hours to prepare, and which yields a tender, sublimely flaky pastry—*perfect* for bouchées.

EQUIPMENT

    ROLLING PIN

    MARBLE PASTRY SLAB OR PLASTIC OR WOODEN CUTTING BOARD

    1¾-INCH FLUTED BISCUIT CUTTER

    1-INCH FLUTED BISCUIT CUTTER

    BAKING SHEETS

    PASTRY BRUSH

INGREDIENTS

1 pound puff pastry, demi-feuilletée, or quick puff pastry, or 1 package frozen puff pastry, thawed 15–20 minutes

Egg wash (1 egg beaten together with 1 teaspoon water)

PREPARATION

Roll out dough to ⅛-inch thickness, then cut out rounds with the fluted 1¾-inch biscuit cutter.

Rinse a baking sheet in cold water, and shake to remove excess. Place half of the pastry rounds on baking sheet, and with the rest, cut a 1-inch round out of the center of each. (It will look like a ring.) Use a pastry brush to moisten the outer edge of a round on the baking sheet with egg wash, then apply a ring on top of it, pressing it down lightly to make it adhere. Repeat until all are attached.

Brush the tops of the circles with egg wash, making sure not to let it drip down the sides of the bouchées.

Bake for 12 minutes, or until golden. Upon removing them from oven, pierce bouchées with the tip of a sharp knife, so the steam can get out and they won't become soggy inside.

These bouchées may be prepared and baked ahead of time and frozen until ready for use. To crisp before using, preheat oven to 400°F, place the bouchées (frozen or not) on a baking sheet in the oven, and immediately turn off the heat. Remove after 5 minutes, and either use warm or let cool to room temperature.

MAKES 32–36 BOUCHÉES.

BRUNOISE, WHICH IS A TINY ⅛-INCH PERFECT DICE, IS ACTUALLY EASY TO ACHIEVE IF YOU KNOW THE TRICK. TO CUT AN ONION INTO BRUNOISE, CUT IT IN HALF, AS SHOWN IN FIGURE A, THEN, WITH A VERY SHARP KNIFE, MAKE VERTICAL CUTS ⅛-INCH APART, BUT NOT CUTTING THROUGH THE ROOT END, WHICH MUST STAY INTACT (FIGURES B AND C). NEXT, STARTING FROM THE BOTTOM, MAKE CUTS PARALLEL TO THE CUTTING BOARD, ⅛-INCH APART, STILL LEAVING ROOT INTACT (SEE FIGURES D AND E). FINALLY, WITH A LARGER KNIFE, SLICE ACROSS ALL YOUR PREVIOUS CUTS, AS SHOWN IN FIGURES F AND G. VOILÀ! YOU'VE ACHIEVED THE BRUNOISE, THE WORLD'S MOST SOIGNÉ GARNISH, AS SHOWN IN THE TRIUMPHANT FIGURE H.

ONION

FIGURE A

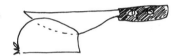

FIGURE B

FIGURE C

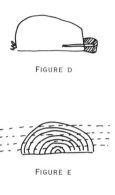

FIGURE D

FIGURE E

FIGURE F

FIGURE G

FIGURE H: ⅛-INCH BRUNOISE

• CAVIAR BOUCHÉES ** •

Caviar Bouchées are perhaps the single most elegant hors d'oeuvre in the entire world, yet once you have the bouchées—tiny puff pastry shells, which you can even buy packaged in gourmet shops—they're among the least time-consuming to prepare. Depending on the caviar prices of the day (I just picked up 2 ounces of Sevruga for $18), they can even be relatively inexpensive, since *one* ounce makes up to 36 bouchées, and few other ingredients are required. They go gorgeously, by the way, with champagne cocktails.

CAVIAR BOUCHÉE

INGREDIENTS

*32–36 puff pastry bouchées
(see preceding recipe, page
110, or purchase in
gourmet shop)*
1 ounce caviar*

*1 cup crème fraîche (see sidebar,
page 114)*
2 bunches chives

PREPARATION

To crisp bouchées that have been made ahead and frozen or refrigerated, or store-bought bouchées, preheat oven to 400°F. Place bouchées on a baking sheet, place in oven, and immediately turn off heat. Let bouchées sit in oven about 10 minutes, until crisp. This may be done the morning

*Use 2 ounces if you're feeling flush, and double the amount on each bouchée. Though they're perfectly elegant with the lesser amount.

of the party, and kept unrefrigerated in an airtight container until ready to use.

Using kitchen shears, snip off the top 2 inches only (the pointy end) of the chives, reserving the rest for another use.

CRÈME FRAÎCHE MAY BE PURCHASED IN THE DAIRY SECTION OF MANY SUPERMARKETS AND FANCY FOOD SHOPS, BUT IT IS INCREDIBLY EASY TO MAKE, AND FAR LESS EXPENSIVE. SIMPLY WHISK TOGETHER EQUAL AMOUNTS OF HEAVY CREAM (NOT ULTRAPASTEURIZED) AND SOUR CREAM. COVER BOWL LOOSELY WITH PLASTIC WRAP, AND LET STAND OVERNIGHT. COVER AND REFRIGERATE UNTIL READY TO USE. FLAVOR CONTINUES TO DEVELOP AS IT SITS REFRIGERATED, AND IT KEEPS FOR ABOUT A WEEK.

ASSEMBLY

Fill bouchées with about a teaspoon of crème fraîche. Top with a small amount of caviar (less than ⅛ teaspoon, which is actually more than you think), and stand up 2 chive ends in the crème fraîche. Serve immediately.

MAKES 36 BOUCHÉES.

VARIATION: SMOKED SALMON BOUCHÉES

Follow directions for Caviar Bouchées, but substitute a small strip of smoked salmon for the caviar. Garnish with a sprig of fennel leaves.

• CRAB BOUCHÉES ** •

Use the best crab you can find for these bouchées, depending on availability in your region. Readers on the West Coast have the sweet and succulent Dungeness crab, which, as far as I'm concerned, is one of our nation's great treasures, and even tastes fresh after it has been frozen and defrosted. Readers on the East Coast will find that lump crabmeat gives the bouchées a marvelously creamy texture.

INGREDIENTS

48 puff pastry bouchées (see recipe, page 110, or purchase in gourmet shop)
½ pound crabmeat, picked over (and chopped finely if it is Dungeness)
1 lemon
2 tablespoons chopped chives

1 avocado
3 tablespoons crème fraîche (see sidebar, page 114)
2 or 3 dashes of Tabasco, or other pepper sauce
Salt and freshly ground white pepper to taste
Chervil leaves for garnish

PREPARATION

Toss the crabmeat with the chives and the juice of half the lemon. Cut the avocado into fine dice, and toss immediately with the juice of the other half of the lemon to prevent discoloring. Add the avocado, crème fraîche, Tabasco, salt and white pepper to crabmeat, and toss until combined, being careful not to crush the avocado. Chill until ready to assemble.

ASSEMBLY

Using a teaspoon, heap a small amount of the mixture into the bouchées. Garnish with a pretty chervil leaf. Serve as soon as possible.

MAKES 48 BOUCHÉES.

VARIATION: LOBSTER BOUCHÉES

Substitute ½ pound diced lobster for crab in the preceding recipe.

• ISLAND CRAB BOUCHÉES ** •

INGREDIENTS

52 puff pastry bouchées (see
   recipe, page 110, or
   purchase in gourmet shop)
½ pound crabmeat, picked over
   (and chopped finely if it is
   Dungeness)
2 limes
1 avocado

1 mango, diced finely
5 scallions, chopped finely
2 or 3 dashes of Tabasco, or
   other pepper sauce
Salt and freshly ground white
   pepper to taste
Chives for garnish, cut into
   2-inch lengths

PREPARATION

Toss the crabmeat with the juice of one of the limes. Cut the avocado into fine dice, and toss immediately with the juice of the other lime to prevent discoloring. Add the avocado, mango, scallions, Tabasco, salt and white pepper to the crabmeat, and toss gently until combined, being careful not to crush the avocado. Chill until ready to assemble.

ASSEMBLY

Using a teaspoon, heap a small amount of the mixture into the bouchées. Stand up 2 chive lengths in each for garnish. Serve as soon as possible.

MAKES 52 BOUCHÉES.

VARIATION: ISLAND LOBSTER BOUCHÉES

Substitute ½ pound finely diced lobster meat for crab in the above recipe.

VARIATION: ISLAND SHRIMP BOUCHÉES

Substitute ½ pound finely diced cooked shrimp in the above recipe.

• CHILLED SHRIMP WITH COCKTAIL SAUCE ** •

This classic is always the most popular hors d'oeuvre at any cocktail party—and it's foolproof! The only setbacks are it can be expensive and you have to shell and devein all the shrimp. Yet the benefits of cooking them yourself are well worth the trouble, since if you buy them precooked, they're bound to be overcooked and tasteless. One pound of medium shrimp will yield 36–40 shrimps; a pound of large will yield 30–36. Don't forget that while medium will go farther and cost a little less, you'll have to devein more. In any case, buy as many as your budget will allow—and don't put them all out at once—because your guests will snap them up!

SHRIMP

INGREDIENTS

For the shrimp:

2 pounds shrimp
4 cups water
4 bay leaves
1 medium onion, sliced
1 carrot, sliced
2 stalks celery, diced

4 teaspoons salt
2 cups dry white wine
1 teaspoon whole black peppercorns
Juice of ½ lemon

For the cocktail sauce:

1 cup ketchup

1 teaspoon Worcestershire sauce

4 dashes Tabasco or other pepper sauce

2 tablespoons horseradish, or to taste*

1 tablespoon lemon juice

PREPARATION

For the shrimp: Peel and devein shrimp; set aside in refrigerator. Place carrot, onion, celery, bay leaves, salt and water in a large kettle, and bring to a boil. Turn down heat, and simmer for 20 minutes. Add the wine and peppercorns, and simmer 5 minutes more. Add the shrimp, and simmer for 2 minutes. Test one for doneness. Do not overcook. Drain shrimp, and chill. Sprinkle with lemon juice.

For the cocktail sauce: Combine all ingredients and chill.

ASSEMBLY

Place cocktail sauce in a small bowl in the center of a large platter. Arrange the shrimp around it, spearing about half of them with frilly toothpicks. Replenish shrimp and sauce as necessary when serving.

MAKES 60–72 LARGE OR 72–80 MEDIUM SHRIMP.

*If using fresh horseradish, which is the most delicious, yet also much more potent than that in a jar, use much less. In fact, even prepared horseradish in jars vary widely in terms of potency, so check carefully for taste.

• CEVICHE TOMATOES ** •

INGREDIENTS

½ pound scallops

Juice of 4 limes

2 jalapeños, seeds removed,
   diced finely

1 bunch scallions, chopped

2 tablespoons chopped cilantro

Salt and cayenne pepper to taste

28 cherry tomatoes

PREPARATION

The night before: Combine the lime juice, jalapeños, scallions, cilantro, salt, and cayenne in a large glass or ceramic bowl. Cut the scallops into small (about ½-inch) pieces. Add to lime juice mixture, and toss to cover. Marinate, covered and refrigerated, overnight.

With a very sharp knife, slice a tiny bit off the bottom of each tomato, so it can stand. Slice off a thin slice from the top, and hollow it out using a small sharp knife or a grapefruit spoon. Turn the tomatoes upside down on a paper towel to drain for about a half hour.

ASSEMBLY

Stuff one or two scallop pieces into each cherry tomato. Serve cold.

MAKES 28 HORS D'OEUVRES.

• CHEESE STRAWS ** •

These go for big dough (get it?) at fancy gourmet shops, and they're not even fresh! How silly, when they're so easy to make.

EQUIPMENT

    ROLLING PIN

    KITCHEN PARCHMENT

INGREDIENTS

2 cups unbleached white flour, plus additional for sprinkling

1 teaspoon salt

¼ cup (½ stick) chilled unsalted butter, cut into small pieces

½ pound freshly grated extra-sharp Cheddar cheese (about 2 cups)

½ cup freshly grated Parmesan cheese, plus additional to sprinkle on top

1 teaspoon Worcestershire sauce

20 grinds of white pepper

¼ teaspoon Tabasco sauce

1 cup milk

PREPARATION

Place flour and salt in the bowl of a food processor, and pulse a few times to combine. Add butter, and process until mixture resembles coarse meal. Add remaining ingredients, and process until the dough forms a ball (it will be sticky). Sprinkle with additional flour, wrap in waxed paper, and refrigerate several hours, or freeze for 30 minutes. *(Note:* Dough may be frozen up to a month at this point, and thawed when ready to bake.)

Preheat oven to 350°F, and line a baking sheet with parchment. On a floured surface, roll out dough to a thickness of ¼ inch. Cut into sticks about 3 inches by ⅜ inch. Sprinkle with Parmesan, and make a couple of twists in each stick, stretching a little as you twist. Place on baking sheet, and bake in the center of the oven 15 minutes, until golden (do not overbake or bottoms will blacken). Turn off oven, and leave to crisp for 30 minutes. Store in an airtight container until ready to use.

CHEESE STRAW

MAKES 120 CHEESE STRAWS.

• CUCUMBER CUPS WITH SMOKED WHITEFISH MOUSSE ** •

EQUIPMENT
> FOOD PROCESSOR OR BLENDER
> ELECTRIC MIXER, EGGBEATER, OR WHISK
> GRAPEFRUIT SPOON OR MELON-BALLER

INGREDIENTS

½ cup heavy cream
½ pound smoked whitefish
2 dashes Tabasco sauce

Freshly ground white pepper
2 hothouse cucumbers
1 bunch chives, finely chopped

PREPARATIONS

For the mousse, remove the skin and bones from the white-fish, and put the fish in the bowl of the food processor or blender. Add the Tabasco and pepper to taste, and process till smooth. (The resulting mixture may be a bit dry.)

Beat the cream until it holds stiff peaks. Stir the fish into the cream, gently but thoroughly. Chill for one to 24 hours.

Cut the cucumbers into 24 ¾-inch slices (do not peel). Reserve any leftover cucumber for another use, or better yet, eat them now, so you don't have to store them. Set the slices flat on a cutting board, and using a grapefruit spoon or a melon baller, scoop out the center of each about ½-inch deep, leaving a base of about ¼ inch to form the bottom of the cup. (Do not break through the bottoms of cups.) Turn the cups upside down on paper towels for 20 minutes to drain. (May be stored covered in refrigerator up to 4 hours, or go to next step, and then store.)

Divide the smoked whitefish mousse among the cucumber cups; garnish with chopped chives. (May be prepared up to this point, and chilled, covered, for up to 4 hours.)

MAKES 24 HORS D'OEUVRES.

HOLLOWED-OUT CUCUMBER SECTION

FILLED WITH MOUSSE

CARROT STICK AND SCALLION
INSERTED

• CUCUMBER GEMS WITH SMOKED SALMON MOUSSE ** •

These stunning gems sound more complicated to prepare than they are. They're cool and delicious—lovely for a summer evening!

EQUIPMENT

    FOOD PROCESSOR OR BLENDER

    ELECTRIC MIXER, EGGBEATER, OR WHISK

INGREDIENTS

½ cup heavy cream
½ pound smoked salmon
2 hothouse cucumbers

2 carrots, peeled and cut into sticks ⅜-inch wide, and 4½ to 5 inches long
6 scallions, trimmed

PREPARATION

For the mousse, place the salmon in the bowl of the food processor or blender, and process till smooth. Beat the cream until it holds stiff peaks. Stir the fish into the cream, gently but thoroughly. Chill for 1 to 24 hours.

In a saucepan, bring about 1 cup salted water to boil, add carrot sticks, blanch 3 minutes, and remove with slotted spoon. Refresh with cold water. Add scallions to saucepan, and blanch 1 minute. Drain and refresh with cold water, and cut each scallion into two pieces (4½ to 5 inches in length).

Cut cucumbers into 4-inch lengths (do not peel). Stand a cucumber section on its end, and using a long, sharp knife, cut out the center, making a hollow ¾ inch to 1 inch in diameter. Repeat for all the sections. Standing them on their ends again, spoon in enough chilled smoked salmon mousse to fill, making sure there are no air pockets. Carefully place a blanched carrot stick in the center of the mousse, and then place a scallion alongside it. Chill for ½ hour to 4 hours.

FINISHED CUCUMBER GEM

ASSEMBLY

Slice filled cucumbers into ½-inch rounds, discarding any uneven ends. Refrigerate, covered, until ready to use, or up to 4 hours.

MAKES 48 HORS D'OEUVRES.

• ENDIVES WITH CHÈVRE * •

INGREDIENTS

4 Belgian endives
11 ounces chèvre (goat cheese)
3 tablespoons walnut oil

Freshly ground black pepper
5 radishes
1 bunch chives, cut finely into
  ⅛-inch pieces

PREPARATION

Cut the root ends off the endives, and separate them into 36 leaves of approximately equal size. Wash and dry. (Reserve the very large and very small leaves for another use.)

Cut the radishes into very thin slices, stack up a few of them, and cut them vertically into matchsticks for garnish.

ASSEMBLY

Place a small amount (about ¾ teaspoon) of chèvre onto the broad, flat end of each endive leaf. Make a small indentation in each with your finger, and pour in a few drops of walnut oil. Grind black pepper over them, sprinkle with chives, and stand up 3 or 4 radish matchsticks in the chèvre.

May be covered with plastic and stored in refrigerator for several hours.

MAKES 36 HORS D'OEUVRES.

• ENDIVES WITH GORGONZOLA AND WALNUT ** •

Try to select a Gorgonzola that isn't terribly blue, or this otherwise gorgeous hors d'oeuvre turns out a weird color.

EQUIPMENT
> FOOD PROCESSOR OR BLENDER
> PASTRY BAG FITTED WITH LARGE STAR TIP (OPTIONAL)

INGREDIENTS

½ pound Gorgonzola or blue cheese
½ pound cream cheese
1 teaspoon Worcestershire sauce
64 walnut pieces
7–8 endives

PREPARATION

In a food processor or blender, combine the Gorgonzola, cream cheese, and Worcestershire sauce, and process until smooth. (May be prepared up to 2 days ahead of time.)

Separate the endive leaves, wash and dry them.

ASSEMBLY

On each endive leaf, pipe or spoon about half a tablespoonful of the cheese mixture. Place a piece of walnut on top.

MAKES ABOUT **64** HORS D'OEUVRES.

• FIRECRACKER ENDIVES *** •

My stepfather invented this by accident in a restaurant when the grilled vegetable salad he had ordered crashed into a plate of endives. It's not only pleasing to the eye—with its tiny parti-colored cubes of vegetables—but healthy and delicious, too. Unfortunately, this summery hors d'oeuvre is impossible to reproduce without either an outdoor or stovetop grill.

EQUIPMENT

OUTDOOR GRILL OR CAST-IRON STOVETOP GRILL

INGREDIENTS

1 ear of corn, shucked

1 medium zucchini, sliced lengthwise into 4 pieces

3 large or 5 medium white mushrooms, each sliced into 2 or 3 slices

1 bunch scallions, trimmed

1 small yellow onion, sliced into thick slices

1 green bell pepper, seeded and cut into eighths

1 red bell pepper, seeded and cut into eighths

5 tablespoons extra virgin olive oil, divided

3 tablespoons red wine vinegar

½ teaspoon salt

¼ teaspoon Dijon mustard

¼ teaspoon cayenne pepper

5–6 Belgian endives, leaves separated

PREPARATION

Light the outdoor grill or barbecue, or heat the stovetop grill on high heat for 5 minutes.

Meanwhile, in a large saucepan, cover the corn with cold water (no salt), and place on the stove over high heat. As soon as water comes to boil, drain corn.

Brush the zucchini, mushrooms, peppers, scallions, onion, and corn with 2 tablespoons of olive oil. Place them on the grill (if you do this on a stovetop grill, you'll have to do it in shifts). Grill the vegetables on both sides until soft and marked with grill marks, but not overly charred. The mushrooms will cook the fastest (about 2–3 minutes on each side, depending on the heat), and the corn will take the longest (about 15 minutes all together) because it has more than 2 sides.

Scrape the corn off the cob into a bowl using a sharp knife. Cut the other vegetables into small dice, about ¼ inch to ⅜ inch, and add to corn.

Prepare a vinaigrette: Combine vinegar, salt, mustard, and cayenne pepper in a small bowl. Whisk in the remaining olive oil drop by drop. Dress the diced vegetables with the vinaigrette. Adjust seasonings. (*Note:* May be prepared to this point up to 1 day in advance.)

ASSEMBLY

Place a teaspoonful of the grilled vegetable salad on each endive leaf. Serve at room temperature.

MAKES 36–40 HORS D'OEUVRES.

• PROSCIUTTO AND MELON WITH PORT-PEPPER SAUCE ** •

A familiar appetizer with an intriguing twist: the luscious warm sauce provides a lovely contrast with the cold melon. This can be made ahead, the morning of the party; the sauce only needs to be reheated briefly before serving.

EQUIPMENT

MELON BALLER (OPTIONAL)

FRILLY TOOTHPICKS

INGREDIENTS

1 ripe cantaloupe

½ pound sliced prosciutto

2 cups ruby port

½ teaspoon freshly ground pepper

PREPARATION

Cut the melon into 1-inch chunks, or use the melon baller to scoop it into balls. Cut the prosciutto into relatively uniform pieces, each just big enough to cover a piece of melon.

For the sauce: Put the port in a small saucepan with the ground pepper, and simmer over a low flame until it is reduced by two-thirds—at the end it should measure about ⅔ cup, and should be almost syrupy.

ASSEMBLY

Wrap each piece of melon in a slice of prosciutto, and secure with a frilly toothpick. Place a small bowl with the warm sauce in the center of a large platter; surround with the wrapped melon pieces to be dipped in the sauce.

MAKES ABOUT 50 HORS D'OEUVRES.

• RADISHES WITH ANCHOVY CREAM * •

EQUIPMENT

> FOOD PROCESSOR OR BLENDER (OPTIONAL)
>
> MELON BALLER
>
> PASTRY BAG FITTED WITH LARGE STAR TIP

INGREDIENTS

32 radishes

8 ounces cream cheese, softened

8 anchovies

PREPARATION

Cut a tiny piece off the bottoms of the radishes so they stand, then cut off the stems on top. Using the small end of a melon baller, scoop out the top of each radish, forming small cups.

Place the anchovies in the bowl of a food processor or blender, and process until smooth (or mash with the back of a fork, or in mortar with pestle). Add the cream cheese, and process until smooth and well combined (or whip together with fork).

ASSEMBLY

Using a pastry bag with a large star tip, pipe a rosette of anchovy cream into each radish. Chill ½ hour, or until ready to serve.

MAKES 32 HORS D'OEUVRES.

• STUFFED CELERY GEMS * •

EQUIPMENT
FOOD PROCESSOR OR BLENDER (OPTIONAL)

INGREDIENTS

8 anchovies

8 ounces cream cheese

Stalks from 2 bunches celery

PREPARATION

Place the anchovies in the bowl of a food processor or blender; process until smooth. Add the cream cheese and process until well blended. (If not using a food processor or blender, you may achieve this by mashing the anchovies, and whipping in the cream cheese with a fork.)

ASSEMBLY

Spoon the mixture into the depression in each celery stalk, letting it heap over a little. Press 2 celery stalks together so they enclose the anchovy cream in between them, and wrap in plastic wrap or wax paper. Repeat until all anchovy cream is used. Chill at least ½ hour, then slice into ½-inch slices. Chill until ready to serve.

MAKES 64 HORS D'OEUVRES.

•   MIRI'S SALAMI TREATS *   •

EQUIPMENT

FRILLY TOOTHPICKS

INGREDIENTS

¼ pound salami, sliced thin at the deli counter
6 ounces cream cheese

Jar of small olives with pimentos

ASSEMBLY

Spoon about ½ teaspoon cream cheese into the center of each slice of salami, then roll it up, and secure it with an olive and a cocktail toothpick with a frilly cellophane hat.

MAKES 25–30 (DEPENDING ON THICKNESS OF SALAMI).

• CHERRY TOMATOES STUFFED WITH
SMOKED TROUT MOUSSE ** •

EQUIPMENT

MELON BALLER OR GRAPEFRUIT SPOON

VERY SHARP PARING KNIFE

FOOD PROCESSOR OR BLENDER

CHILLED MIXING BOWL AND WHISK OR ELECTRIC MIXER

PASTRY BAG FITTED WITH LARGE DECORATIVE TIP

INGREDIENTS

24 cherry tomatoes
½ cup heavy cream
*1 small smoked trout, about ½
    pound*

2 dashes Tabasco sauce
Freshly ground white pepper
1 bunch chives, finely chopped

PREPARATION

Cut a tiny slice off the bottom of each tomato, so it will stand up. Then cut about ¼ of the top off each. Using the melon baller, scoop out the seeds. Turn the tomatoes upside down on a paper towel to drain for a few minutes.

For the mousse, remove the skin and bones from the trout, and put the fish in the bowl of the food processor or blender. Add the Tabasco and pepper to taste, and process till smooth. (The resulting mixture will be dry.)

Beat the cream until it holds stiff peaks. Stir the fish

into the cream, gently but thoroughly. Chill for 1 to 24 hours.

ASSEMBLY

Using the pastry bag, pipe a portion of mousse into each tomato. Garnish with a sprinkling of finely chopped chives.

MAKES 24 HORS D'OEUVRES.

VARIATION

Use smoked salmon mousse (recipe follows), or other smoked fish mousse instead of smoked trout mousse.

• SMOKED SALMON MOUSSE * •

This may be used in place of smoked trout mousse in cherry tomatoes (see previous recipe). Or spread it onto just about any canapé base, and garnish with pretty sprigs of fennel leaves or dill.

EQUIPMENT
>FOOD PROCESSOR OR BLENDER
>CHILLED MIXING BOWL AND WHISK OR ELECTRIC MIXER

INGREDIENTS

½ cup whipping cream
¼ pound smoked salmon
2 dashes Tabasco sauce

2 dashes Worcestershire sauce
Freshly ground white pepper to taste

PREPARATION

Place the smoked salmon, Tabasco, Worcestershire sauce and white pepper in the bowl of the food processor or blender, and process until smooth.

Beat the cream until it holds stiff peaks. Gently fold in the fish mixture until well combined. Chill 1 to 24 hours.

MAKES ABOUT 1 CUP.

• AN-MY'S SUMMER ROLLS *** •

These Vietnamese summer rolls are among the freshest, most
delicious morsels in the world—and my friend An-My exe-
cutes them better than anyone else. We modified her recipe
into tiny hors d'oeuvre-size rolls, but try them again one
night when you're not throwing a cocktail party, for a first
course for dinner. To do so, simply leave the spring roll skins
whole, and roll up the ingredients tightly inside, as you
would a burrito. But be careful—they're highly addictive.

All the preparation for these rolls may be accomplished
the morning of the party, and the sauce may be prepared the
night before, leaving only the assembly for the afternoon of
the party.

INGREDIENTS

1 pound pork shoulder, cut in
   half
1 pound medium shrimp
1 onion, sliced
2 carrots, sliced
2 stalks celery, diced
½ package rice stick noodle
   (Chao Ching)*

1 package large spring roll
   skins*
1 head red leaf lettuce, torn
   into salad-size pieces
1 bunch mint, stems removed
1 bunch cilantro, stems removed
2 bunches chives, cut into
   3-inch lengths

*Available in Asian groceries.

For Dipping Sauce:

¾ *cup hoisin sauce**

*2 tablespoons peanut butter
    (smooth)*

2 teaspoons sugar

¼ *cup water*

1 tablespoon plum sauce*

*Dried red peppers to taste
    (optional)*

1 tablespoon chopped peanuts

PREPARATION

In a large kettle, add onion, carrots, and celery to 3 quarts of salted water. Bring to a simmer, turn down heat, and simmer 15 minutes. Add pork, and cook for ½ hour, or until meat is no longer pink inside. Remove pork with tongs, strain the broth and return it to the kettle, keeping it just barely simmering.

While pork cools, peel and devein shrimp. Turn heat under broth to medium, add shrimp, and cook for 1 minute. Drain shrimp.

Remove fat and skin (if any) from pork, and cut into ⅛-inch slices, about 1½ inches by ¾ inches. Slice shrimp in half along their length.

Cook the rice stick noodle in 3 quarts of salted water for about 8 minutes, or until it is cooked through. Drain and rinse in cold water to prevent sticking.

(*Note:* All of the above steps may be performed as early as the morning of the party, and kept chilled until ready to assemble.)

*Available in Asian groceries.

For sauce: Combine all ingredients except chopped peanuts in a small saucepan, and cook on a low flame, stirring, until the sugar is dissolved. *(Note:* May be prepared up to this point as early as 24 hours in advance, and reheated when ready to use.) Garnish with chopped peanuts.

ASSEMBLY

Have ready a dish of warm water next to a cutting board or work board, and all your prepared summer roll ingredients lined up in front of you. Using scissors, cut the large round spring roll skins into small squares, 4 by 4 inches. Dip one of them into the water for about 5 seconds, and place on work surface. Place on it, to the right or left of the center, a lettuce leaf, several cilantro and mint leaves, a teaspoonful of rice stick noodle, half a shrimp, and a slice of pork. Fold up a flap on the bottom, then roll tightly, leaving top open. It may seem like it doesn't want to stick, but lay it seam side down on a platter, and it will. As you work, cover the finished ones with a damp paper towel. When they're done, stand them up and garnish them by inserting a 3-inch length of chive into the center of each.

To serve, place the dipping sauce in a small bowl in the center of a large platter, and surround with the summer rolls.

MAKES 60–70 ROLLS.

• REGALITOS *** •

Regalo is the Spanish word for "gift"; I call these "regalitos" because each one looks like a little tiny present, all tied up with a grilled scallion "ribbon." Regalitos are truly a case of the whole being greater than the sum of the parts—they just consist of a mini corn tortilla filled with guacamole, but the result is incredibly fresh, tasty, and delicious. Choose the bumpy, black Hass avocados for the greatest flavor. To make the tortillas, I tried a tortilla press, but since these need to be very thin, it actually doesn't work as well as the simple method I use here. This may appear to be time-consuming, but I actually made 32 of them in less than 45 minutes, and the guacamole is very quick.

EQUIPMENT

> AN OUTDOOR GRILL OR A STOVETOP GRILL OR A CAST-IRON SKIL-LET
>
> A GRIDDLE OR A COMAL (TORTILLA GRIDDLE) OR A CAST-IRON SKILLET
>
> MORTAR AND PESTLE OR A MOLCAJETE OR A BOWL AND WOODEN SPOON
>
> ROLLING PIN
>
> KITCHEN PARCHMENT OR WAX PAPER
>
> A 3-INCH ROUND BISCUIT- OR COOKIE-CUTTER

INGREDIENTS

For the mini-tortillas:

1 cup masa (available in the
    flour section of many
    grocery stores)

½ cup warm water

For the scallion "ribbons":

2 bunches scallions

Salt

Juice of ½ lime

For the guacamole:

2 tablespoons chopped grilled
    scallion bottoms (you'll get
    them from the 2 bunches of
    scallions that you'll grill
    for the "ribbons")

1 ripe avocado

3 tablespoons chopped cilantro

2 seeded and finely chopped
    jalapeño or serrano peppers

⅓ cup finely chopped fresh
    tomato

Juice of ½ lime

½ teaspoon salt

PREPARATION

For the scallion "ribbons": Trim and wash the scallions. Place
them on a heated grill or skillet, sprinkle with a squeeze of
lime, a little salt, and cook for 3–5 minutes, then turn them
over, sprinkle with more salt and lime juice, and continue another 3–5 minutes, until they're floppy.

Cut the scallions into two pieces each—the bottom or
white part should be 3 to 4 inches long, and the top, or
green part, should be 6 to 7 inches long. Chop up the white
part and reserve it for the guacamole. Using your fingers,
separate each green part into 3 or 4 strands. You'll need

about 30 all together, but do a few more just for good measure. Set aside.

For the tortillas: Have ready a bowl lined with a large cloth
napkin or dishtowel. As the tortillas are done, put them in
here and keep them covered and they'll stay soft and steamy
for quite a while.

Heat the griddle, *comal* (tortilla griddle), or cast-iron
skillet on a medium-high flame. While it's heating, mix together the masa and the warm water in a mixing bowl.

Lay down a sheet of parchment on top of a cutting
board, then form a small ball of tortilla dough (about 1½
inches), flatten it slightly, place it on the parchment, and
place another piece of parchment on top of it. Roll it out to
a very thin circle, roughly 4 inches in diameter. Remove the
top parchment, and using the biscuit or cookie cutter, cut out
a 3-inch circle. Slide the circle off the parchment, onto the
hot griddle, and cook for about 1 minute, until the edges just
start to curl up. Flip it over, cook for another minute, and
put it in the cloth-covered bowl. This all happens much more
quickly than it sounds, and soon you'll form a rhythm where
you're forming the next tortilla while the first one is cooking,
and then you'll have 2 or 3 cooking at a time. Continue until
all the dough is used up.

To make the guacamole: Crush the scallion whites, cilantro, chili
peppers, and salt in the mortar or *molcajete,* or chop them very
finely together, and put them in the bowl. Cut the avocado
in half, scoop out the flesh, and mash it in the mortar
or in the bowl with the back of a wooden spoon until it's

fairly smooth. Stir in the tomato and lime juice, and season to taste.

BEFORE ROLLING AND TYING

ASSEMBLY

Lay out three or four tortillas, place one teaspoonful of guacamole in the center of each, roll it up into a little cylinder, and tie it up with a grilled scallion green, making a knot at the top. These will stay fresh covered with plastic, but not refrigerated, for up to five hours.

MAKES 30 REGALITOS.

FINISHED REGALITO

• SPICED ALMONDS * •

Spiced Almonds and the Curried Cashews that follow are delicious and easy treats; they'll be snatched up practically as soon as you put them out—even if you double the recipe! Either recipe works with either almonds or cashews—in fact, try any raw nuts—peanuts, hazelnuts, Brazil nuts—and experiment with your favorite spices.

INGREDIENTS

½ pound raw almonds
½ teaspoon sea salt
1 teaspoon cumin
1 teaspoon ground coriander
    seed

¼ teaspoon ground cardamom
2 tablespoons olive oil

PREPARATION

To blanch the almonds, pour enough boiling water over them to cover, let stand for about 3 minutes, and drain. The skins should come off easily between your fingers.

Heat the olive oil in a sauté pan, add blanched almonds, and sauté on a low flame for 30 minutes, until golden. Meanwhile, mix together the cumin, coriander, cardamom, and salt. When the almonds are done, drain on paper towels, place in a bowl, add spice mixture, and toss to coat. Almonds are ready when cool. May be stored in an airtight container for up to a week.

• CURRIED CASHEWS ˚ •

INGREDIENTS

½ pound raw cashews　　　　　*½ teaspoon sea salt*
2 tablespoons olive oil　　　　*Dash of cayenne pepper*
2 teaspoons curry powder

PREPARATION

Heat the olive oil in a sauté pan. Add the cashews and sauté on low heat for about 20–25 minutes, until golden.

Meanwhile, combine the curry powder, salt, and cayenne. When the cashews are done, drain on paper towels. Add the curry mixture, and toss to coat. Cashews are ready to serve when cool. May be stored in an airtight container for up to a week.

HOT HORS D'OEUVRES AND CANAPÉS

• THE BEST AND EASIEST PASTRY ** •

I adapted this following version of the classic French *pâte brisée* from the one taught to me by Danièle Mazet Delpeuch, formerly the private chef to French President François Mitterand, and now a *cuisinière* and cooking educator in Dordogne and New York. It's easy, quick, and sublimely light and flaky—and if it's good enough for Monsieur le Président, it's good enough for me.

Use it to make tiny tart shells (see recipe following), which can be filled with an unlimited number of savory fillings, or make quichelettes, following one of the barquette filling recipes that follow on pages 156–58 (as these tart shells are much smaller than barquettes, you'll get about twice as many hors d'oeuvres).

Or use it to make barquettes (instructions follow on page 154). Though they're a little bigger than most of the hors d'oeuvres in the book, requiring consumption in *two* bites (for most people), the barquette is a classic shape, and now and then it's nice to have something one can really sink one's teeth into.

EQUIPMENT

FOOD PROCESSOR (OPTIONAL)

INGREDIENTS

1¼ cups unbleached white
    flour
1 teaspoon salt
Pinch of sugar

7 tablespoons unsalted butter,
    well chilled
1 egg, slightly beaten
1 tablespoon milk

PREPARATION

Put the flour, salt, and sugar in the bowl of the food processor, and pulse a few times to combine. Cut the butter into
small pieces, and drop them into the flour mixture. Process
a few seconds, until mixture resembles coarse meal. (If you
don't have a food processor, you may do this in a large bowl,
using pastry blender or two forks.) Combine the milk and
egg, and add to flour mixture. Pulse 5 times, then process
until dough forms into a large ball. (If you do this by hand,
make a well in the middle of the flour, add the egg and milk,
and use a wooden spoon to combine, then knead until
smooth.) Wrap pastry in a cloth, and chill for at least 2
hours.

• TINY TART SHELLS ** •

EQUIPMENT

>   ROLLING PIN
>   2-INCH FLUTED BISCUIT CUTTER
>   1 OR 2 MINI-MUFFIN TINS

TINY TART SHELL

INGREDIENTS

One recipe The Best and
*   Easiest Pastry (page 149)*

Nonstick cooking spray

PREPARATION

Preheat oven to 350°F. Spray the mini-muffin tin with a light coating of nonstick spray.

Roll out dough to ⅛-inch thickness, and cut out rounds with the biscuit cutter. Use scraps to form another ball, roll out again, and cut out more rounds. Push a round, which will be slightly larger than the bottom of a mini-muffin shape, into the tin, pressing it gently into the corners. It will have the shape of a little tiny pie crust. Repeat until tin is full.

Bake for 10–12 minutes, or until golden. Unmold, and repeat, until all the rounds are baked.

Tiny tart shells may be frozen until ready for use. Simply reheat them in 350°F oven for about 5 minutes, let cool to room temperature and fill. Or, if making quichelettes, simply let them thaw 10 minutes, then fill and bake as directed.

MAKES ABOUT 40 TART SHELLS.

• PISSALADIETTES ** •

These tiny onion tarts—molded after the larger *pissaladière* from the south of France—must be tried to be believed. The onions are cooked very slowly, till they're meltingly soft and sweet; when they're baked, the flavor of thyme, and the saltiness of the olives and anchovies complete the happy synergy.

INGREDIENTS

PISSALADIETTE

40 Tiny Tart Shells (page 151)
4 medium onions, sliced very thin
3 tablespoons extra virgin olive oil
Salt and pepper to taste

2 teaspoons fresh thyme
8–10 anchovies, cut into 40 thin slices
20 niçoise olives, pitted

PREPARATION

Heat olive oil in a sauté pan. Add onions, salt and pepper, and cook on a very low flame, stirring occasionally, 35–40 minutes, or until very soft and sweet. Do not let brown.

Preheat oven to 350°F.

ASSEMBLY

Place a small spoonful of onions into each tiny tart shell. Sprinkle with thyme leaves. Garnish half of them with a niçoise olive, and half with two anchovy slivers placed in an X. Bake for 20 minutes.

MAKES 40 TARTLETS.

• CRAB TARTLETS ** •

INGREDIENTS

*36 Tiny Tart Shells (page
    151)*
*½ pound lump crabmeat,
    picked over*
1 teaspoon lemon juice
1 egg, beaten

*1 tablespoon finely chopped
    parsley*
*¼ cup grated Parmesan cheese
    (plus 2 tablespoons for
    sprinkling on after)*

PREPARATION

Preheat oven to 350°F. Toss crabmeat with lemon juice. In a
mixing bowl, combine crabmeat, egg, parsley, and Parmesan
cheese. Mix well.

ASSEMBLY

Line up tiny tart shells on an ungreased baking sheet. Place
a small spoonful of the crab mixture in each, and sprinkle a
little more Parmesan over each.

Bake 15–17 minutes, or until Parmesan is toasty-brown.

MAKES 36 TARTLETS.

• BARQUETTE SHELLS ** •

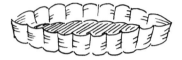

BARQUETTE MOLD

Barquettes, which are shaped like tiny boats, may be filled with any one of many different types of savory fillings as their "cargo." Barquettes do break the cocktail party rule that says finger food must be able to be eaten in one bite; most people will eat them in two. But I've included them anyway because they're so classic and cute, and the delicious fillings in the recipes that follow hold together well, ensuring that the barquettes won't fall apart and embarrass your guests.

EQUIPMENT

    BARQUETTE MOLDS, PREFERABLY NON-STICK (USE AS MANY AS
        YOU HAVE, BUT PREFERABLY AT LEAST EIGHT)
    BAKING SHEET
    ROLLING PIN
    PIE WEIGHTS OR DRIED BEANS

INGREDIENTS
One recipe The Best and
Easiest Pastry (page 149)

PREPARATION
Preheat oven to 350°F. First use half of the dough and keep the other half chilled. Roll out dough to ⅛-inch thickness. Cut out, using barquette molds as a guide, leaving ½ inch all around, except at points. Fit into molds, turning edge under and pressing into molds. Chill in refrigerator for 20 minutes.

Prick the bottom of each a few times with a fork, and place a few pie weights or dried beans in each. Place molds on baking sheet, bake for 10 minutes, let cool slightly, then unmold. Repeat as needed until dough is all used. May be stored frozen for several months.

MAKES 24–26 BARQUETTES, READY FOR FILLING.

• MUSHROOM BARQUETTES ** •

INGREDIENTS

24–26 Barquette Shells (page 154)

10 ounces fresh white mushrooms, sliced thin

½ ounce dried porcini mushrooms

1 tablespoon olive oil

2 tablespoons unsalted butter

1 tablespoon fresh thyme

2 eggs

2 tablespoons milk

Salt and freshly ground pepper

PREPARATION

Soak dried porcinis in ½ cup boiling water for ½ hour. Drain, reserving liquid for another use.

Heat butter and olive oil in a sauté pan on a low flame. Sauté fresh mushrooms for 5 minutes, then add the drained porcinis, thyme, and salt and pepper to taste. Continue cooking for about another 5 minutes, until the fresh mushrooms give up their water.

Meanwhile, lightly beat the eggs and the milk together with ¼ teaspoon salt. Remove the mushrooms from heat, cool slightly, and add egg mixture.

Preheat oven to 350°F.

ASSEMBLY

Spoon mixture into barquette shells, place them on an ungreased baking sheet, and bake for 15–17 minutes, until pastry is golden. Serve warm.

MAKES 24–26 HORS D'OEUVRES.

• LEEK BARQUETTES ** •

INGREDIENTS

24 Barquette Shells (page 154)

4 large leeks, white part only, sliced thin (about 4 cups)

3 tablespoons unsalted butter

2 eggs

1 tablespoon milk

Salt and freshly ground white pepper

1 egg, beaten with 2 teaspoons water, for pastry glaze

PREPARATION

Melt the butter in a sauté pan, add the leeks, and sauté on a low flame for 30 minutes, until leeks are very tender. Add salt and white pepper to taste. Let cool completely.

Beat the eggs together with the milk. Add the leeks, and combine well.

Preheat oven to 350°F.

ASSEMBLY

Brush the edges of the barquette shells with egg glaze, then fill each shell with a spoonful of the leek-egg mixture. Place shells on an ungreased baking sheet, and bake 15–17 minutes, until pastry is golden. Serve warm.

MAKES **24** HORS D'OEUVRES.

• GOAT CHEESE AND SUN-DRIED TOMATO BARQUETTES ** •

INGREDIENTS

24–26 Barquette Shells (page 154)

2 ounces sun-dried tomatoes (not packed in oil)

8 ounces chèvre (goat cheese)

2 eggs

1 egg, beaten with 2 teaspoons water, for pastry glaze

Salt and freshly ground white pepper

PREPARATION

Pour 1 cup boiling water over the sun-dried tomatoes, and soak for 20 minutes. Drain, saving water for another use. Chop the tomatoes into small pieces, place in a medium bowl, and combine with the goat cheese, eggs, salt, and pepper.

Preheat oven to 350°F.

ASSEMBLY

Brush the edges of the pastry with egg glaze, and fill each barquette shell with a spoonful of the cheese mixture. Place the shells on an ungreased baking sheet, and bake for 15 minutes. Serve warm.

MAKES 24–26 HORS D'OEUVRES.

• MINI HAM AND CHEDDAR BISCUITS * •

These can be made in no-time flat, yet they're heartwarming-ly tasty.

EQUIPMENT

FOOD PROCESSSOR OR BLENDER
ROLLING PIN
1½-INCH ROUND BISCUIT CUTTER

INGREDIENTS

2 cups Bisquick
½ cup milk
¼ teaspoon Tabasco sauce

1 cup grated Cheddar cheese
½ pound baked ham

PREPARATION

Preheat oven to 450°F. Place the ham in the bowl of the food processor or blender, and process until chopped as finely as possible.

Place the Bisquick in a large bowl, pour in the milk and Tabasco, and stir with a wooden spoon until almost combined. Add ham and Cheddar, and combine well.

Roll out dough on a floured surface to ½-inch thickness. Cut out biscuits with cutters, place on an ungreased baking sheet, and bake for 8–10 minutes, until golden brown.

MAKES 56 BISCUITS.

• SAGE AND CORN BEIGNETS ** •

INGREDIENTS

1 cup yellow cornmeal
½ cup unbleached flour
1 teaspoon salt
¼ teaspoon freshly ground
    white pepper
1 teaspoon baking powder
2 tablespoons sugar

1 small bunch fresh sage,
    roughly chopped (about ⅓
    cup)
2 ears fresh corn
½ cup milk
2 eggs, slightly beaten
24 ounces canola, sunflower, or
    safflower oil

PREPARATION

Place first 7 ingredients in a mixing bowl, and combine well. Using a sharp knife, cut the kernels off the corncobs, and add them to the cornmeal mixture. Add the milk and eggs, and stir until combined.

Heat the oil in a deep skillet until very hot, but not smoking. To test, drop a tiny amount of batter in oil; if it sizzles and rises to the surface right away, it's hot enough. Drop the batter by teaspoonfuls into oil—do not crowd. (You'll fry in several batches.) Fry a minute or two until golden on bottom, then turn over with a slotted spoon and fry another minute until golden brown. Drain on paper towels.

MAKES 64 HORS D'OEUVRES.

• POTATO PUFFS ** •

Simple as these may be, my boyfriend says they're the best hors d'oeuvre in the book! The plain ones are simple, yet elegant, and the variations that follow are fantastic. If you're having a Columbus Day or other Italian theme party, try all three variations, which, together on a serving platter, represent red, white, and green—the colors of the Italian flag.

POTATO PUFF

EQUIPMENT

    KITCHEN PARCHMENT

    POTATO RICER OR FINE SIEVE

    ELECTRIC MIXER OR WHISK

    PASTRY BAG FITTED WITH LARGE STAR TIP

INGREDIENTS

2 Idaho (russet) potatoes
2 egg whites
½ teaspoon salt

Freshly ground white pepper to
   taste
⅓ cup heavy cream

PREPARATION

Preheat oven to 400°F. Line a baking sheet with parchment.

    Peel and slice the potatoes, and boil them in salted water until tender, about 20 minutes. Drain and put through potato ricer, or mash them through a sieve, using the back of a wooden spoon. Beat in cream, add salt and white pepper.

    Beat the egg whites in a small bowl until they hold stiff

PIPING MIXTURE INTO STARS

161

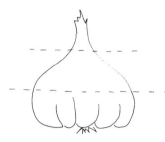

CUT HERE, DISCARD TOP END

WRAP THESE PIECES IN FOIL

peaks. Stir half of the egg whites gently into the potatoes, then gently fold in the rest, using a rubber spatula.

Using the pastry bag fitted with a large star tip, pipe the mixture onto the parchment-lined baking sheet into 1½-inch round stars.

Bake for 17–20 minutes, until the ridges of the stars are brown, while the rest remains white.

MAKES 44 HORS D'OEUVRES.

VARIATION: ROASTED GARLIC POTATO PUFFS

INGREDIENTS

Same as for Potato Puffs, plus:
2 heads garlic
2 teaspoons olive oil

Additional salt and freshly ground pepper, to taste

PREPARATION

Preheat oven to 350°F. Cut the garlic heads in half horizontally, drizzle with olive oil, salt and pepper, wrap in foil, and bake for about 1 hour. When cool enough to handle, squish the garlic out of its skins—it will be like a paste. To make it extra-smooth, pass it through a sieve. Follow instructions for Potato Puffs above, adding the roast garlic paste along with the cream.

VARIATION: SUN-DRIED TOMATO POTATO PUFFS

INGREDIENTS

Same as for Potato Puffs, plus:
2 ounces sun-dried tomatoes
(dry, not packed in oil)

PREPARATION

Pour 1 cup boiling water onto the sun-dried tomatoes, and let stand for 20 minutes. Drain, reserving soaking water for another use. Puree the tomatoes in a blender or food processor, and pass through a fine sieve. Follow instructions for Potato Puffs above, and add the sun-dried tomato paste along with the cream. Proceed as above.

VARIATION: BASIL OR PARSLEY POTATO PUFFS

INGREDIENTS

Same as for Potato Puffs, plus: *⅓ cup very finely chopped basil*
or parsley

PREPARATION

Prepare as for Potato Puffs, stirring in the herbs along with the cream. Proceed as in recipe.

• SHRIMP TOAST ** •

These pupu platter standards are spectacularly delicious with cocktails, and they're quick and easy as well, unless you're afraid of frying. In that case counseling may be available in your area. Shrimp toast are best served immediately, but they're still very good if you fry them ahead of time, keep them covered in the fridge, and reheat for 5 minutes in a 300°F oven. They may also be frozen, and popped right into a preheated 325°F oven for 15 minutes.

EQUIPMENT

    FOOD PROCESSOR (OPTIONAL)

    LOTS OF PAPER TOWELS

INGREDIENTS

½ pound raw shrimp, shelled and deveined

3 tablespoons chopped water chestnuts

1 teaspoon minced ginger root

1 tablespoon slightly beaten egg

1 teaspoon cornstarch

2 teaspoons soy sauce

⅓ cup sesame seeds

10 slices white bread

About 24 ounces peanut oil, or enough to fill a skillet about one inch

PREPARATION

Cut the crusts off the slices of bread and set aside (up to a few hours) to let them dry out a little.

    Finely chop shrimp, together with water chestnuts and

ginger, or combine them in the bowl of the food processor and pulse 8–10 times until finely chopped (do not overprocess). Stir in the soy sauce, egg, and cornstarch, and combine well.

ASSEMBLY

Spread the mixture onto the pieces of bread, and cut each one into quarters (half of them in square shapes, and half in triangles). Pour the sesame seeds onto a small plate. Take one of the squares, and press it, shrimp paste side down, into the sesame seeds. Repeat for half the squares and half the triangles; leave the rest plain. (*Note:* May be prepared up to this point up to 2 hours before serving. Wrap in plastic and keep refrigerated.)

Heat the oil until very hot, but not smoking. To test, drop a few bread crumbs in—they should sizzle right away. Fry the squares and triangles, a few at a time, by lowering them paste side down with a slotted spoon into the oil. Fry until golden brown, 1 minute or less, then flip them over, and fry for just a few seconds on the other side. Drain on paper towels.

MAKES 40 HORS D'OEUVRES.

• TIKI DRUMETTES ** •

INGREDIENTS

24 chicken wings, or wing
"drumettes," if your butcher
has them
2 cups bottled teriyaki sauce
½ cup red wine vinegar

2 inches ginger root, minced
(about 4 tablespoons)
4 cloves garlic, minced
1 tablespoon hot Chinese
mustard

CUT HERE

FINISHED DRUMETTE

USE THIS PART FOR STOCK,
OR GIVE TO CAT

166

PREPARATION

To cut chicken wings into "drumettes," cut off the largest part at the joint with a cleaver or heavy knife according to illustration, and holding the joint at the top, scrape down the meat with a smaller knife, exposing about an inch and a half of the bone. (Save the rest of the wing parts for stock.)

To make the marinade, combine the teriyaki sauce, vinegar, ginger, garlic, and mustard in a large glass or ceramic bowl. Add the drumettes, and marinate in refrigerator at least 1 hour, or overnight.

Preheat oven to 400°F. Place drumettes in baking dish, and bake for 25 minutes, basting every few minutes with the marinade. Remove from oven, and turn oven up to broil.

Place drumettes on broiler pan, and broil 3 minutes on each side. Serve hot.

MAKES 24 HORS D'OEUVRES.

VARIATION: BARBECUE CHICKEN DRUMETTES

Substitute a bottle of your favorite barbecue sauce for the marinade in the above recipe, marinate at least 1 hour, and cook the same way; or better yet, finish on the barbecue instead of the broiler.

• JERK DRUMETTES •

"Jerk" is a marinade popular in Jamaica, used for pork as well as chicken. To get the full benefit of the intense flavor, marinate the drumettes for 24 hours before cooking.

EQUIPMENT
FOOD PROCESSOR OR BLENDER

INGREDIENTS

24 chicken wings, or wing
"drumettes," if your
butcher has them
1 Scotch bonnet pepper (or 4
jalapeños), seeds removed
1 clove garlic, peeled
¼ cup fresh lime juice
1 teaspoon salt

1 onion, quartered (chopped, if
using blender)
¼ cup dark brown sugar
¼ teaspoon ground cloves
1½ teaspoons ground allspice
2 teaspoons fresh thyme (or 1
teaspoon dried)
⅓ cup vegetable oil

PREPARATION

For 1 cup of marinade: Turn on the food processor, and drop in the Scotch bonnet pepper and garlic. Add the lime juice and salt, and process a few seconds. Add the onion, brown sugar, cloves, allspice, and thyme, and process until smooth. With processor still running, pour in the vegetable oil, and process until combined.

Following the directions and illustrations for the Tiki Drumettes (page 166), cut the chicken wings into drumettes.

Place in glass or ceramic container, coat well with marinade, cover, and refrigerate for 24 hours.

Preheat oven to 400°F. Place the drumettes in a baking dish, and bake for 25 minutes, basting every few minutes with the marinade. Remove from oven, and turn oven up to broil.

Place drumettes on broiler pan, and broil 3 minutes on each side. Serve hot.

MAKES 24 HORS D'OEUVRES.

• SWEET AND SOUR MEATBALLS ** •

EQUIPMENT

FRILLY TOOTHPICKS

INGREDIENTS

1 pound ground pork
1 bunch scallions
1 cup sliced water chestnuts
½ cup bread crumbs
2 teaspoons soy sauce
2 teaspoons minced ginger root
Freshly ground white pepper
4 tablespoons peanut oil

1 cup unbleached white flour
6 cups homemade chicken stock,
  or 2 13-ounce cans chicken
  broth, with enough water
  added to make 6 cups
1 recipe Sweet and Sour Sauce
  (recipe follows)

PREPARATION

In a mixing bowl, combine the first seven ingredients. Wet hands, and form into 1-inch balls.

Heat 2 tablespoons peanut oil in a skillet. Place flour on a plate, dredge meatballs, shake off excess flour, and brown in skillet, shaking pan to brown on all sides (do not crowd). Remove to a bowl as meatballs are browned, and continue, adding more oil to skillet as necessary. (*Note:* May be prepared up to this point and stored refrigerated up to 6 hours in advance.)

Heat the chicken stock in a large saucepan. Drop in meatballs and cook for 20 minutes. Place on a warmed platter, with a decorative toothpick in each, and pass with a small bowl of Sweet and Sour Sauce.

MAKES 72 MEATBALLS.

• SWEET AND SOUR SAUCE • •

INGREDIENTS

⅓ cup sugar

⅓ cup white vinegar

⅓ cup water

2 teaspoons cornstarch,
   dissolved in 2 teaspoons
   water

⅓ cup pineapple or apricot
   preserves

PREPARATION

Bring sugar, vinegar, and water to a boil. Stir in the cornstarch mixture, and cook on a low flame for 5 minutes, or until thickened. Stir in the preserves, and simmer 5 more minutes. Serve warm or at room temperature. *(Note:* May be prepared and stored refrigerated up to 24 hours in advance. To serve, simply allow to warm to room temperature, or reheat briefly in a saucepan.)

• STILTON AND PORT CANAPÉS * •

INGREDIENTS

1½ cups ruby port
1 baguette

1 pound Stilton cheese

PREPARATION

Pour the port into a saucepan, bring to a boil, reduce heat, and simmer 15–20 minutes or until reduced by more than two-thirds, to measure between ⅓ cup and ½ cup. (*Note:* May be done day before and reheated.)

Preheat oven to 350°F. Slice the baguette into 32 ½-inch slices. Place on baking sheet, and toast for 10 minutes. (May be sliced the day before and stored in an airtight container.)

Slice Stilton into 32 pieces. It'll be crumbly, but that's okay. (May be done the day before and stored in an airtight container.)

ASSEMBLY

Spread a piece of Stilton onto each slice of toasted baguette. Drizzle a little port sauce over each. Serve immediately.

MAKES 32 CANAPÉS.

• MOZZARELLA BITES * •

INGREDIENTS

1 pound fresh mozzarella
½ cup sun-dried tomatoes
 (packed in olive oil,
 drained)

1 baguette

PREPARATION

Preheat broiler.

Slice baguette into rounds, about ⅜-inch thick. Slice mozzarella into 24 pieces about ⅜-inch thick. Each slice should fit comfortably on a baguette round. Cut the sun-dried tomatoes into julienne shreds.

ASSEMBLY

Place a piece of mozzarella on a baguette slice, and top with a few shreds of the sun-dried tomato. Run under the broiler for about 1 minute, until cheese is melty.

MAKES 24 CANAPÉS.

• SARDINE CANAPÉS ** •

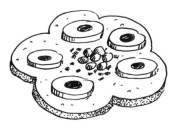

SARDINE CANAPÉ DECORATED WITH A
PAPRIKA FISH

GARNISHED WITH OLIVE SLICES AND
CAPERS

EQUIPMENT

FOOD PROCESSOR OR BLENDER

ROUND, OVAL, DIAMOND-SHAPED, OR OTHER COOKIE OR BISCUIT
CUTTERS, ABOUT 2 INCHES, OR A SHARP KNIFE

A PIECE OF PAPER WITH A ¾-INCH FISH SHAPE CUT OUT, TO STEN-
CIL A PAPRIKA DESIGN AS GARNISH (OPTIONAL)

INGREDIENTS

2 loaves white bread
2 cans sardines in olive oil,
drained
⅓ cup finely chopped parsley
For garnishes:
Green olives stuffed with
pimentos, thinly sliced
Finely chopped raw shallots
Lemon zest

2 tablespoons fresh lemon juice
4 tablespoons mayonnaise
1 teaspoon Worcestershire sauce
Freshly ground black pepper

Paprika
Capers
Finely chopped parsley

PREPARATION

Remove the crusts from the bread, slice lengthwise into
½-inch slices, if not already sliced, and lightly toast enough
for 40 canapés.

While they're toasting, prepare the spread. Place sardines, parsley, lemon juice, mayonnaise, Worcestershire sauce,
and pepper in the bowl of a food processor or blender, and
process until smooth.

174

ASSEMBLY

Spread each slice with a layer of sardine mixture, and cut out shapes using the biscuit or cookie cutters or a sharp knife. Garnish with a border of parsley. For an attractive touch hold the fish stencil over each canapé, and drizzle paprika over it. Remove the stencil, and you'll see a paprika fish. Or garnish with a few shreds of lemon zest and a few capers, or olive slices in a flower shape with a border of shallots, or any other combination you like.

These are best when made no more than 3 or 4 hours before serving (store them covered in plastic in the fridge until ready to serve).

To serve, run them under a preheated broiler for 1 or 2 minutes.

MAKES 40 CANAPÉS.

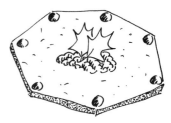

GARNISHED WITH SHALLOTS, PARSLEY, AND CAPERS

GARNISHED WITH LEMON ZEST AND OLIVE SLICES

SCALLOP BROCHETTE LACED WITH
BACON

• SCALLOP BROCHETTES LACED WITH BACON ** •

These tasty tidbits may be prepared almost entirely in the morning. Place the assembled skewers on a plate, covered with plastic wrap, and store in refrigerator. Broil or grill just before serving.

EQUIPMENT

    30 6-INCH BAMBOO SKEWERS

INGREDIENTS

½ pound sea scallops

½ pound bacon, each slice cut in half lengthwise

30 cherry tomatoes

¼ cup fresh lime juice, plus enough rice vinegar to make ⅓ cup

⅓ cup Thai or Vietnamese fish sauce

⅓ cup sugar

1½ inches of ginger root, peeled and minced

¼ teaspoon red pepper flakes

1 clove garlic, minced

PREPARATION

If you're using large scallops, cut each into 4 pieces. You should end up with about 30 all together. For the marinade, combine lime juice/vinegar, fish sauce, sugar, ginger, red pepper, and garlic in a glass or ceramic bowl. Add the scallops,

176

and marinate, refrigerated, for 1 to 3 hours. Meanwhile, soak the skewers in cold water for 1 hour.

Cook the bacon in a skillet until done, yet not crisp. Drain on paper towels.

ASSEMBLY

Preheat broiler, or heat grill.

On a skewer, pierce one end of a bacon strip, then a scallop, then the middle of the same piece of bacon, then a cherry tomato, then the end of the bacon. The bacon should be laced in and out of the scallop and tomato. Repeat until all ingredients are used.

Broil or grill for 2 minutes on each side.

MAKES 30 BROCHETTES.

• GRILLED GINGER-LIME SHRIMP WITH PEANUT DIPPING SAUCE ** •

I have a wonderful little cast-iron stovetop grill, which makes dishes like this a breeze. Otherwise, either grill the shrimp outside on the barbecue, run them under a broiler, or sauté them briefly in a skillet.

EQUIPMENT

    STOVETOP OR OUTDOOR GRILL, OR BROILER, LARGE SKILLET OR SAUTÉ PAN

    40 6-INCH BAMBOO SKEWERS

INGREDIENTS

1 pound medium raw shrimp
   (36–40 shrimp)
For the marinade:
Juice of 2 limes
2 teaspoons soy sauce
For the dipping sauce:
⅓ cup peanut butter
Juice of 1 lime
1 teaspoon sugar
½ teaspoon soy sauce
1 teaspoon finely minced ginger
   root

1 tablespoon olive oil (or less)
   for grilling or sautéing

1 tablespoon minced ginger root
½ cup extra virgin olive oil

¼ teaspoon red pepper flakes
½ teaspoon Asian sesame oil
¼ cup water

PREPARATION

To make marinade, mix together the lime juice, soy sauce, and ginger in a medium bowl. Whisk in the olive oil in a steady stream. Peel the shrimp, leaving their tails on, and devein. Add shrimp to marinade in bowl, toss to coat, cover with plastic, and leave in refrigerator for about 2 hours.

To prepare peanut dipping sauce, whisk together the lime juice and sugar in a small bowl, then whisk in soy sauce, ginger, and red pepper flakes. Stir in the peanut butter and water, then whisk in the sesame oil. Make at least an hour ahead of time so flavors have time to emerge.

If using a grill, soak the skewers in cold water for 1 hour.

Just before serving, brush the stovetop grill with a little olive oil, and heat grill for 5 minutes on high heat, or prepare outdoor barbecue for grilling. Meanwhile, spear each shrimp on the end of a skewer. When grill is hot, turn heat to medium, and grill shrimps about 1 minute on each side, or until opaque. (If using a skillet, heat olive oil on medium-high heat, then sauté shrimp for about 1½ minutes on each side, or until opaque. When finished, spear each through twice on a skewer.)

To serve, place dipping sauce in the center of a platter. Arrange skewered shrimp around sauce in a spokelike formation, with the skewers radiating out from the center.

MAKES 36–40 HORS D'OEUVRES.

• HOT VINEGARED SHRIMP ** •

My friend An-My invented this easy and delicious hors d'oeuvre.

EQUIPMENT

FRILLY TOOTHPICKS

INGREDIENTS

1¼ pounds medium shrimp
½ cup plus 1 tablespoon extra virgin olive oil
Juice of ½ small lemon, plus enough red wine vinegar to make ¼ cup

½ teaspoon soy sauce
⅓ cup chopped cilantro
Salt and red pepper flakes to taste

PREPARATION

Peel and devein the shrimp. In a small bowl, add the soy sauce to the vinegar and lemon juice. Whisk in the ½-cup olive oil. (These two steps may be done up to 6 hours ahead of time. Store shrimp, covered, in refrigerator.)

Heat 1 tablespoon olive oil in sauté pan until hot, but not smoking. Add the shrimp, and sauté quickly, sprinkling with salt and red pepper flakes, about 1 minute on each side. Remove to bowl.

Pour the vinaigrette into the sauté pan, and cook for about 2 minutes, reducing by half. Add the shrimp and cook for 15 more seconds, then add cilantro, and cook for a few seconds.

ASSEMBLY

Pour the sauce left in the pan into a small bowl, and place it in the center of a serving platter. Heap the shrimp around it, inserting fanciful toothpicks in each.

MAKES ABOUT 40 HORS D'OEUVRES.

• GRILLED ROSEMARY SHRIMP * •

EQUIPMENT

STOVETOP OR OUTDOOR GRILL, OR BROILER

32 9-INCH BAMBOO SKEWERS

INGREDIENTS

For the rosemary oil:

½ cup rosemary leaves, roughly chopped

1 cup high-quality extra virgin olive oil

For the shrimp:

1 pound large shrimp

1½ tablespoons fresh lemon juice

⅛ teaspoon salt

PREPARATION

One to several days before the party, make the rosemary oil. Place the olive oil and rosemary in a small saucepan. Heat till just below a simmer, turn down the flame to very low, and warm gently for 8 minutes. Let cool, then steep overnight in refrigerator. Line a sieve with cheesecloth, and strain the oil through it into a clean jar or bottle. (*Note:* Oil will keep for up to 3 weeks in refrigerator.)

Soak the skewers in cold water for 1 hour.

Peel and devein the shrimp, leaving their tails intact. In a glass or ceramic bowl, combine the lemon juice and salt. Whisk in ⅓ cup of rosemary oil, then add the shrimp. Cover with plastic, and marinate, refrigerated, for 15–20 minutes.

Place 1 shrimp on each skewer, and place on hot grill (or under broiler). Grill 1½ minutes, brush with marinade, and turn over. Grill another 1½ minutes, or until opaque.

MAKES ABOUT 32 HORS D'OEUVRES.

• GRILLED CAMARONES * •

EQUIPMENT

STOVETOP OR OUTDOOR GRILL, OR BROILER

32 9-INCH BAMBOO SKEWERS

INGREDIENTS

For the marinade:

⅓ cup freshly squeezed lime juice
½ teaspoon salt
1 clove garlic, chopped

1 jalapeño pepper, chopped
*1 cup high-quality extra virgin
olive oil*

For the shrimp:

1 pound large shrimp

PREPARATION

Soak the skewers in cold water for 1 hour.

Combine the lime juice, salt, jalapeño, and garlic in a ceramic or glass mixing bowl. Whisk in the olive oil. Peel and devein the shrimp, leaving their tails intact. Place the shrimp in the marinade, cover, and refrigerate for 20 minutes.

Place 1 shrimp on each skewer, and place on hot grill (or under broiler). Grill 1½ minutes, brush with marinade, and turn over. Grill another 1½ minutes, or until opaque.

MAKES ABOUT 32 HORS D'OEUVRES.

• GRUYÈRE PUFFS ** •

Don't be intimidated by these elegant little cheese puffs—
they're incredibly easy, and practically foolproof. There are
two tricks involved: one, be sure to dump in all the flour at
once; and two, make sure the eggs are room temperature. The
puffs are based on the classic recipe for cream puffs, or in
French, *pâte à choux (choux* means "cabbage"—these little
guys are actually more like brussels sprouts in size and
shape).

INGREDIENTS

¼ *cup unsalted butter (½*
   stick)
½ *teaspoon salt*
1 *cup unbleached white flour*
4 *whole eggs (room*
   temperature)

1 *egg white (room temperature)*
1 *cup grated Gruyère cheese*
½ *cup finely grated Parmesan*
   cheese

PREPARATION

Preheat oven to 400°F. Line 2 or 3 baking sheets with parchment.

Bring 1 cup water to a boil in a medium saucepan with
the butter and salt. When the butter's completely melted, remove from heat, and add the flour all at once. Stir briskly
with a wooden spoon until the dough forms a ball. Make a
well with the spoon in the middle of the dough, add one of

the eggs, and beat with the wooden spoon. The consistency will be exceedingly strange at first—pieces of the dough will slide off of each other—but in about half a minute, the consistency will become uniform. Add each egg separately, beating until the consistency is uniform, then add the egg white, and beat until smooth and glossy. Beat in the cheeses.

Using a teaspoon, drop small spoonfuls (about ¾ inch in diameter) of the mixture onto the baking sheet, leaving about 1 inch between them. You should be able to fit at least 24 on each sheet.

Bake for 10 minutes, then turn down oven to 350°F, and bake another 20 to 25 minutes, until the puffs are hard.

As soon as you take them out, make a small incision in each puff with a small sharp knife to release the steam (and prevent them from getting soggy inside).

Serve immediately, or cool and freeze them, reheating them for about 3 minutes in a 350°F oven.

MAKES ABOUT 70 CHEESE PUFFS.

VARIATION: HAM AND CHEDDAR PUFFS

INGREDIENTS

Same as for Gruyère Puffs, but substitute aged Cheddar for Gruyère, omit Parmesan, reduce butter to 2 tablespoons, and add 1 cup (about ⅓ pound) chopped ham.

PREPARATION

Same as for Gruyère Puffs. Stir in ham along with cheese.

• MODERN MEATBALLS ** •

EQUIPMENT

DO MAKE SURE EVERYONE

IS TALKING TO SOMEONE

AND HAS A DRINK.

FOOD PROCESSOR, BLENDER, OR IMMERSION BLENDER

FAT SEPARATOR (OPTIONAL)

FRILLY TOOTHPICKS

☾

INGREDIENTS

5 shallots (about 1 cup, sliced thin)

2 tablespoons olive oil

½ pound lean ground beef

½ pound ground veal

3 tablespoons finely chopped parsley

1 small carrot, peeled and chopped finely

½ red bell pepper, chopped finely

½ green bell pepper, chopped finely

1 shallot, chopped finely

1 tablespoon capers, drained

1 teaspoon fresh thyme, chopped finely

1 whole egg plus 1 egg white, beaten

2 cups homemade meat stock (or 1 13¾-ounce can meat broth, plus enough water to make 2 cups)

Bouquet garni of 1 bay leaf, 3 sprigs thyme, and 3 sprigs fresh parsley, tied into a cheesecloth bag

½ teaspoon paprika

Salt and freshly ground pepper to taste

PREPARATION

Heat the olive oil in a sauté pan, add the sliced shallots, and sauté on very low heat for ½ hour. Set aside. (*Note:* May be prepared up to 24 hours ahead of time and stored covered in the refrigerator.)

Combine the two meats, the peppers, chopped shallot and carrot, chopped thyme and parsley, capers and eggs, ½ teaspoon salt, and freshly ground pepper. Wet hands and form into small meatballs about 1½ inches in diameter. (May be prepared up to 8 hours ahead of time and stored covered in the refrigerator.)

Place the sautéed shallots in a large sauté pan, and stir in the stock or broth. Add the bouquet garni, paprika, and salt and pepper to taste. Bring to a boil, add the meatballs, and when cooking liquid returns to a boil, turn down to low heat. Simmer, covered, for 35 minutes.

Remove the meatballs to a platter, and keep warm in a 250°F oven. Remove the bouquet garni, and strain all the fat off the top of the cooking liquid—a fat separator works best for this. Puree the defatted cooking liquid together with the cooked shallots, using a food processor, blender, or immersion blender. Taste for seasoning.

Pour the sauce into a small bowl, and place in the center of a large platter. Arrange the meatballs around it, placing a frilly toothpick in each.

MAKES ABOUT 55 MEATBALLS.

• CRISPY HAM AND ASPARAGUS ROLLS
WITH COGNAC-CITRUS
DIPPING SAUCE *** •

This hot hors d'oeuvre is a winner—and much less complicated to prepare than it might appear. The textures of the
ham and the asparagus are terrific with the light crispness of
the phyllo, and the tangy sauce accompanies it perfectly.

EQUIPMENT
    BAKING SHEET
    KITCHEN PARCHMENT
    PASTRY BRUSH

INGREDIENTS
For the ham and asparagus
    rolls:
½ pound Black Forest ham,
    thinly sliced
1 pound asparagus

1 package phyllo dough, left in
    refrigerator overnight or
    thawed for 2–3 hours
4 tablespoons unsalted butter

For the sauce:
1 tablespoon unsalted butter
2 tablespoons finely chopped
    shallots
Juice of 1 lemon
Juice of 1½ oranges

2 tablespoons cognac
¼ teaspoon salt
1 tablespoon sugar

PREPARATION

To prepare the sauce, melt the butter in a small saucepan, add the shallots, and cook them on a low flame until soft, about 5 minutes. Add the cognac, salt and sugar, and turn the heat to medium. Cook for 1 minute. Add the orange and lemon juices, and cook for another 2 minutes. Set aside until ready to reheat for use.

FIGURE A

For the rolls: Line a baking sheet with parchment, and preheat oven to 400°F, if they're to be served right away. If not, you can store them on the lined baking sheet.

FIGURE B

   Trim the woody ends off the asparagus, then steam for 5 minutes. Run cold water over them or plunge them into ice water to stop cooking. They should be quite firm, since they'll cook a little more in the oven. Set aside.

   Melt 4 tablespoons butter; set aside.

FINISHED PRODUCT

ASSEMBLY

Carefully unroll the phyllo dough, remove a few sheets, and with a sharp knife, cut them into quarters—they should measure about 9 by 6 inches.

   On a clean, dry surface, place 1 sheet of phyllo. Brush the surface lightly with melted butter, and place another sheet on top of it. Brush the surface of the second lightly with butter, then place a third on top.

   With the phyllo horizontally in front of you, place a layer of ham in the center of the sheet, reaching all the way to the left and right edges, but leaving at least 1 inch of

191

dough on the top and bottom. You may have to trim the ham to make it fit.

Next place 3 asparagus spears in the center of the ham, then trim 3 others to fit next to them so asparagus extends all the way to the left and right edges, as shown in Figure A. Grab the bottom edge, and roll the whole thing tightly, keeping the asparagus in the center. Brush the far edge with butter, and seal the roll. It should now look like Figure B. Slice into 1¼-inch pieces, and place, seam down, on the parchment. Repeat until all of the ham and asparagus are used up.

Bake for about 15 minutes, or until golden. While they're baking, reheat the sauce. Place the sauce in a small bowl in the center of a platter, and arrange the rolls around it.

MAKES 28 HORS D'OEUVRES.

•   STAMP 'N' GO **   •

Versions of this Jamaican favorite are served all over the Caribbean. With rum or cachaça drinks, they're irresistible.

INGREDIENTS

½ pound salt cod
¾ cup unbleached white flour
1 teaspoon freshly grated lime
   peel
⅛ teaspoon allspice
½ teaspoon salt
4 scallions, chopped
2 jalapeños, chopped finely, or
   1 teaspoon finely chopped
   habañero chiles

1 egg, lightly beaten
¼ cup milk
Peanut oil—enough to fill
   skillet to ½ inch
2 limes, cut in quarters

PREPARATION

The night before: Place the cod in a large bowl, cover with cold water, and soak overnight, changing the water 2 or 3 times.

Drain the cod, place in a medium saucepan, cover with water, bring to boil, and simmer 20 minutes. Drain, and flake with a fork, removing any bones and skin. Set aside.

Mix the flour, lime peel, allspice, and salt in a large mixing bowl. Make a well in the center, and into it pour the egg and milk. Mix with a wooden spoon until blended, then add the cod, scallions, and chili peppers.

Heat the oil in a skillet until hot but not smoking,

about 350°F. Drop batter by teaspoonfuls into the hot oil, and fry 1½ to 2 minutes on each side, until golden brown. Drain on paper towels.

Keep warm in a 300°F oven until all are finished. Place on a platter, and squeeze lime wedges over them.

MAKES 30 HORS D'OEUVRES.

• COCONUT SHRIMP ** •

INGREDIENTS

1 pound medium shrimp
¾ cup unbleached white flour
⅛ teaspoon salt
½ cup coconut milk

¼ cup fresh lime juice
1 egg
2–3 dashes Tabasco sauce
2 cups shredded sweetened coconut
24 ounces canola or safflower oil

PREPARATION

Peel and devein shrimp. Combine the flour, salt, coconut milk, lime juice, egg, and Tabasco in the bowl of a food processor or blender. Process until blended. Alternatively, they may be whisked together in a bowl. Scrape the batter into a mixing bowl, and add the shrimp.

Heat the oil in a skillet until very hot, but not smoking. To test, drop a few shreds of coconut into the oil. If it sizzles and rises to the surface right away, it's hot enough.

Spread out some of the coconut on a plate. Take a shrimp out of the batter, shake off the excess batter, and press both sides of shrimp into the coconut. Drop into oil; repeat for 4 or 5 others. Cook 2–3 minutes, or until golden brown. Remove with a slotted spoon and drain on paper towels. Repeat until all shrimps are used.

MAKES 36–40 HORS D'OEUVRES.

• SHRIMP AND HEARTS OF PALM EMPANADAS WITH MANGO-LIME DIPPING SAUCE ** •

EQUIPMENT
2¾-INCH ROUND BISCUIT CUTTER
PASTRY BRUSH

INGREDIENTS

*1 recipe The Best and Easiest
   Pastry (page 149)*
*½ pound shrimp, peeled,
   deveined, and chopped*
3 scallions, chopped
½ cup chopped hearts of palm
⅛ teaspoon salt

3–4 dashes Tabasco sauce
1 egg, beaten
*Egg wash (1 egg, beaten with
   1 teaspoon water)*
*1 cup mango-lime dipping
   sauce (recipe follows)*

PREPARATION
Preheat oven to 375°F. In a mixing bowl, combine the shrimp, scallions, hearts of palm, salt, Tabasco, and egg.

ASSEMBLY
Roll out the dough to ⅛-inch thickness, and stamp out circles using the biscuit cutter. Place about ½ teaspoon of shrimp mixture in the center of each, fold in half, and press edges together. To seal, press down hard on the edges, using a fork.

196

Place on a lightly buttered baking sheet, brush tops with egg wash, and bake 15 minutes, or until golden brown. *(Note:* May be prepared up to this point and frozen. To reheat, bake in a 350°F oven for 10 minutes.)

MAKES 36 EMPANADAS.

• MANGO LIME DIPPING SAUCE ˙ •

This fresh, tangy sauce goes gorgeously with Coconut Shrimp, as well as Shrimp and Hearts of Palm Empanadas.

EQUIPMENT
>   FOOD PROCESSOR OR BLENDER

INGREDIENTS

2 ripe mangos
2 habañero chiles (or 1 jalapeño), seeds removed

Juice of 1 lime
2 tablespoons brown sugar

PREPARATION

Cut the mangos as close to the pits as possible, score the flesh on both sides, and cut the fruit off of the peel. Peel the portion with the pit, and remove as much fruit from it as possible.

Turn on the food processor, drop in the habañero chiles one at a time, and process. Place the rest of the ingredients in the bowl of a food processor, and process until smooth.

MAKES 1 CUP DIPPING SAUCE.

• ALBONDIGAS ** •

These little meatballs, the ones usually served in the Mexican soup bearing the same name, are tender and tasty. Mince the vegetables as finely as possible to ensure a smooth texture.

EQUIPMENT

FRILLY TOOTHPICKS

INGREDIENTS

⅓ cup finely minced green pepper

1 small carrot, peeled and minced finely

1 jalapeño pepper, seeded and minced finely

½ cup finely minced onion

2 cloves garlic, minced finely

2 tablespoons olive oil

1 pound lean ground beef

1 egg, slightly beaten

2 tablespoons cooked white rice

2 tablespoons finely chopped parsley

1 teaspoon salt

Freshly ground black pepper to taste

6 cups homemade beef stock, or 2 13¾-ounce cans of beef broth, with enough water added to make 6 cups

2 bay leaves

PREPARATION

Combine the first 5 ingredients in a small bowl. Heat the olive oil in a sauté pan, and sauté minced vegetables on a low flame until soft, about 5 minutes. Let cool slightly.

In a large saucepan, bring beef stock and bay leaves to a simmer.

In a mixing bowl, combine the ground beef, egg, rice, salt, pepper, parsley, and sautéed minced vegetables. Form gently into 1¼-inch balls.

Drop half of the meatballs into the beef stock, and simmer gently for 10 minutes. Remove with a slotted spoon. Repeat for the remainder of the meatballs. (*Note:* May be prepared ahead up to this point the day before. Store meatballs, covered, in the refrigerator. Strain stock through a cheesecloth-lined sieve, reserve, and refrigerate separately. When ready to serve, remove hardened fat from stock, bring to a simmer in a large saucepan, and heat through, 2 or 3 minutes.)

ASSEMBLY

Arrange the albondigas on a platter with a decorative toothpick stuck into each. Keep the rest warm by letting them sit in the barely simmering broth until ready to serve.

MAKES 62 HORS D'OEUVRES.

• SHREDDED PORK SOPITAS *** •

Sopes are thick little corn tortillas with a ridge around the edge. In Mexico, they're filled with a wide variety of ingredients, and eaten as an appetizer. This recipe makes very small ones, hence the name "sopitas." Once you get into the rhythm of rolling them and pinching up the sides, they'll begin to go very quickly. And it's fun—like playing with Play-Doh, only it tastes better! You can use your imagination and fill them with whatever alternative ingredients you like—any combination of grilled chicken, pinto beans or black beans, cheese, small strips of steak, salsa verde . . . the possibilities are endless.

INGREDIENTS

For the pork:
3 pounds pork shoulder, or   *2 bay leaves*
   other inexpensive cut   *1 teaspoon salt*
For the sopitas:
2 cups masa*   *1 tablespoon butter, if reheating*
1 cup warm water

*Cornmeal flour prepared with lime. Available in supermarkets, usually in the flour section, but sometimes in the international section, or in any Mexican grocery.

For the salsa:

*1 large ripe tomato, chopped
  finely (just over 1 cup)*
*⅓ cup finely chopped white
  onion*
*2 jalapeño peppers, seeded and
  diced finely*

Juice of ½ lime
2 tablespoons chopped cilantro
*Additional cilantro leaves for
  garnish*

PREPARATION

For the pork: Remove any skin from the pork, and cut off the bone, if any. Cut into 2-inch pieces, keeping the fat. Place in a large skillet, barely cover with water, and add salt and bay leaves. Bring to a boil, turn heat to medium, and simmer, uncovered, stirring occasionally, until water evaporates, about 1½ hours. At this point, with the water gone, the pork will begin to fry. Turn the flame to low, and continue cooking, stirring occasionally, until pork is very tender, about another hour.

When the meat has cooled, cut off the fat, and shred the meat using a fork and a small sharp knife. (May be prepared up to 1 day ahead of time. Store refrigerated in an airtight container, and bring to room temperature before using, or warm briefly in oven.)

For the sopitas: Combine the masa and warm water in a mixing bowl. Form into a ball, and cover with a damp cloth. Heat a griddle, an ungreased skillet, or, if you happen to have one, a *comal* (used for cooking tortillas) on medium heat.

Pinch off an amount of dough the size of a walnut, and

roll into a ball between your palms. Using a rolling pin, flatten it on a board to make a circle 2 inches in diameter. Using your fingers, push up the sides of the circle to form a little "retaining wall"—the sopita should now be 1½ inches in diameter. Make 5 or 6 of them, then place them flat side down on the hot griddle. Cook 1 minute, then flip with spatula. The cooked side should be golden, with little spots of brown. Press down lightly on the sopitas with the spatula, then leave to cook 1 more minute. Remove to cool. Repeat until all dough is used. Store refrigerated in an airtight container, up to 6 hours, or until ready to use.

For salsa: Stir together ingredients, and adjust seasoning. (May be prepared up to 4 hours ahead of time.)

ASSEMBLY

To reheat sopitas, preheat oven to 350°F. Place a tiny amount of butter in the depression of each, place on an ungreased baking sheet, and warm about 5 minutes.

Place a small amount of shredded pork (about 1 teaspoon) in the center of each, and top with 1 teaspoon salsa. Garnish with a pretty cilantro leaf.

MAKES 48 SOPITAS.

6

COCKTAILS AND OTHER
YUMMY DRINKS

THE COMBINING AND
MANIPULATING OF
NATURE'S POTENT
FERMENTS IN
PREPARATION FOR ACTION
UPON THE HUMAN SYSTEM
SHOULD NOT BE TREATED
AS A MERE MATTER OF
ROUTINE.
   —HARMAN BURNEY BURKE
(BARNEY BURKE), IN BURKE'S
   COMPLETE COCKTAIL AND
   TASTYBITE RECIPES, 1936

☾

Once you get the hang of it, mixing drinks is a snap. Figure on three drinks per person average, have one bottle of soda water or mineral water for every three or four people (depending on the crowd) and chances are you shan't run out of drinks. Cocktails usually contain one and a half ounces of liquor, which is the size of the large part of a jigger (the small side, the "pony," is one ounce), and the jigger is what you'll use for mixing one or two drinks at a time. But when you mix drinks in larger quantities, you may find it easier to use an eight-ounce (one cup) Pyrex measuring cup, which is calibrated conveniently in ounces on the side. A fifth of spirits contains enough for sixteen or seventeen cocktails, so three bottles will yield fifty drinks.

Mix martinis, Manhattans, old-fashioneds, and the like in a martini pitcher. Fill it with ice, add the spirits (and the vermouth, bitters if called for, etc.), stir with a glass rod or long bar spoon, and pour. If your pitcher doesn't have a spout that catches the ice, you'll need to use a cocktail strainer.

For drinks containing fruit juice, such as daiquiris, margaritas, and mai tais, and for drinks with a syrup, shaking them vigorously over ice in a cocktail shaker is the quickest way to get them cold and thoroughly mixed—without letting them get watery. If you use one with a screw-top pouring spout, you won't need a cocktail strainer when you pour.

This is not to say one can't shake martinis—one can. The idea that the gin might be "bruised" by shaking is a myth—think of it—what's to bruise? You don't, however, want to shake anything with soda or tonic in it, for obvious reasons.

If you're serving cocktails on the rocks, use fresh ice in the glass. And don't let it get too melty in the ice bucket. Have plenty of it on hand, and refresh the bucket periodically.

You may notice that I haven't included any blender drinks—such as frozen margaritas, daiquiris and piña coladas—because they're noisy and messy—altogether too inelegant for a cocktail party as soigné as yours will be. Anyway, in my book, those three are even better *not* frozen. But if you adore them frozen, of course you'll have to have them. You're on your own.

Some people use superfine sugar to sweeten their cocktails, since it dissolves more readily than regular granulated. I prefer to use simple syrup, which mixes perfectly and instantaneously (see sidebar, page 214).

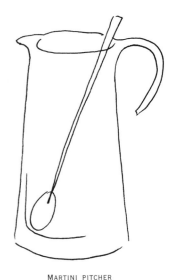

MARTINI PITCHER

COCKTAIL SHAKER

GARNISHES

A TWIST

TWIST IT OVER THE COCKTAIL

LIME

LIME, BEFORE TRIMMING

LIME, TRIMMED

Prepare all the garnishes you need beforehand, though not too early or the citrus will dry out. Two or three hours before the party is fine. Just before cutting them, wash the citrus fruit. Cover citrus garnishes with a damp paper towel, and refrigerate until ready to use; others may be covered with plastic wrap and chilled.

Salt or Sugar Around the Rim: Pour salt or sugar into a small dish, rub a lemon or lime around the rim of a glass, and dip the rim in the dish. Be sure to do this before you pour, or guess what—the cocktail will fall out! Also, don't do it too early or the garnish will be soggy.

Twist: This means a strip of the yellow part of a lemon peel, with as little of the white pith as possible. Some people use a small, sharp paring knife to cut off a section of peel; others use a sharp vegetable peeler. Either way, trim them into uniform strips, 1/4–3/8 inch in width and 1–1 1/2 inches long. To garnish, twist it over the cocktail, releasing the aromatic lemon oil into the drink, and drop it in.

Lemon Peel Knot: This is similar to a twist, only it's 3 or 4 inches long and 1/4-inch wide. Tie a single knot in the middle. Some people claim to use a wide end of a lemon zester to achieve a piece of zest this long, but I've never found one sharp enough to work.

Lime: "Garnish with lime" means cut a lime in half lengthwise, then cut four or five wedges from each half. Trim the sides (as in the illustration) for easy squeezing, and make a straight cut to remove the pith and membrane in the center.

SLICE OF ORANGE

Slice of Orange, Lemon, or Lime: Slice the citrus horizontally *(not through the stem and navel end)* about ⅜-inch thick, then cut the slice in half. Remove any seeds.

Squeeze of Lemon or Lime: Prepare as for lime, above, but squeeze it as you drop it in the drink.

Olive: Use either one big green olive stuffed with a pimento, speared on a wooden toothpick with a frilly cellophane hat, or two small ones impaled on same. Have them all set up in a dish beforehand, even if it seems like it doesn't take long to do them for each drink.

COCKTAIL ONIONS

Cocktail Onion: Use right out of the jar. Spear one or two on a wooden toothpick with a frilly cellophane hat in your favorite color.

Maraschino Cherry: Use the ones with stems, please, and just drop 'em in, unless pairing with other garnishes.

MARASCHINO CHERRY

207

GLASSWARE

A stemmed cocktail or martini glass will work for most cocktails served "up," and a six-ounce old-fashioned glass will suit most on-the-rocks drinks. But sometimes an unorthodox glass can be festive as well—for instance, if you happen to have a grillion wine goblets, they might serve as on-the-rocks glasses for a nice change.

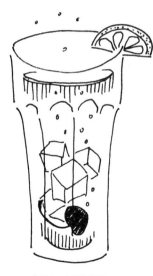

A WELL-GARNISHED
ALCOHOL-FREE DRINK

THE ALCOHOL-FREE ZONE

Take as much care with the alcohol-free drinks you serve as you do with the cocktails. For instance, spring for a swanky mineral water rather than club soda ordinaire, and do select one or two of the delectable alcohol-free concoctions herein.

If you happen to be the proud owner of a juicer, you're in fat city. Use it to prepare your favorite vegetable juice combinations—they go great with hors d'oeuvres—and squeeze up some tempting exotic fruit juices, which will be wonderful mixed with sparkling mineral water.

A little imagination goes a long way, so long as you pay attention to the appearance of your alcohol-free drinks, and take care to choose a pretty garnish. Who knows? You may even tempt someone to fall *onto* the wagon!

COCKTAILS

• MARTINI (EXTRA DRY) •

This is the martini as we have come to worship it—ultradry, with just a whisper of vermouth. Use top-quality gin, such as Bombay or Tanqueray, and a good imported vermouth, either Cinzano or Boissière.

Trickle of dry vermouth   *2 ounces gin*

Pour vermouth into an ice-filled martini pitcher, and then pour it out, leaving only the vermouth that coats the ice. Add the gin, stir well, and strain into a martini glass. Garnish with olive.

DO NOT LET ANYONE DRIVE DRUNK.

☾

• GIBSON •

Trickle of dry vermouth   *2 ounces gin*

Pour vermouth into an ice-filled martini pitcher, and then pour it out, leaving only the vermouth that coats the ice. Add the gin, stir well, and strain into a martini glass. Garnish with a cocktail onion.

• DRY MARTINI •

For 2 drinks: *1 ounce dry vermouth*
5 ounces gin

Pour into an ice-filled martini pitcher, stir well, and strain into martini glasses. Garnish with olives.

• TRADITIONAL MARTINI •

When martinis were first put upon this earth, this was the recipe for a "Dry Martini." Though out of style, it's still delicious.

3 ounces gin   *1 ounce dry vermouth*

Pour over ice in a martini pitcher, stir well, and strain into a martini glass. Garnish with an olive.

• BLUEBERRY MARTINI •

¼ ounce vermouth   *1 ounce blueberry juice**
3 ounces gin   *Squeeze of lemon*

*Use juice extractor, or blend fresh blueberries in a food processor or blender, and strain through a sieve lined with cheesecloth.

Pour the vermouth over ice in a cocktail shaker just to coat the ice; pour out excess. Add the gin, blueberry juice, and a squeeze of lemon; shake well, and strain into a martini glass. Garnish with 3 blueberries and a twist of lemon skewered on a cocktail toothpick.

• GIMLET •

In my book, a gimlet is always gin, never vodka, and always uses fresh lime juice, rather than bottled. Anyone with a sweet tooth should double the simple syrup.

1½ ounces gin
1 ounce freshly squeezed lime
  juice

½ ounce simple syrup (see
  sidebar, page 214)

Pour ingredients into an ice-filled cocktail shaker, shake well, and strain into a martini glass. Garnish with a slice of lime.

• PINK LADY •

2 ounces gin
4 dashes grenadine

¼ ounce egg white

Shake ingredients vigorously over ice; strain into a sherry glass. Garnish with a maraschino cherry.

• BRONX COCKTAIL •

1 ounce gin   ½ ounce dry vermouth
½ ounce sweet vermouth   Juice of ¼ orange

Shake over ice in a cocktail shaker. Strain into a stemmed martini glass; garnish with a slice of orange and a maraschino cherry.

• OLD-FASHIONED •

1 sugar cube   2 ounces bourbon
3 dashes bitters

Place the sugar cube in bottom of an old-fashioned glass. Sprinkle with bitters, add ice, pour in bourbon, and stir. Garnish with a slice of orange, a maraschino cherry, and a lemon peel.

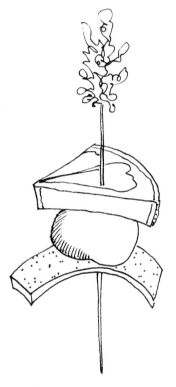

GARNISH FOR OLD-FASHIONED

• MANHATTAN •

1½ ounces rye or bourbon   Dash bitters
½ ounce sweet vermouth

Shake over ice in a cocktail shaker; strain into a stemmed cocktail glass, and garnish with a maraschino cherry.

• ROB ROY •

1½ ounces Scotch whiskey   *¾ ounce sweet vermouth*

Pour over ice into a martini pitcher, stir, and strain into a stemmed cocktail glass, or over ice in an old-fashioned glass. Garnish with a maraschino cherry.

• PERFECT ROB ROY •

2 ounces Scotch whiskey   *½ ounce dry vermouth*
½ ounce sweet vermouth

Pour over ice into a martini pitcher, stir, and strain into a stemmed cocktail glass, or over ice in an old-fashioned glass. Garnish with a twist.

• BATCH OF MINT JULEPS •

For 5 drinks:
20–25 sprigs of fresh mint   *8 ounces (1 cup) bourbon*
2 tablespoons superfine sugar

Fill 5 tall glasses with crushed ice. In a cocktail shaker, muddle the mint with the sugar and a teaspoon of water. Add the

213

bourbon, shake, and strain into the ice-filled glasses. Garnish with sprigs of mint.

TO MAKE SIMPLE SYRUP:
COMBINE TWO PARTS SUG-
AR AND ONE PART WATER
(FOR INSTANCE, ONE CUP
SUGAR AND HALF A CUP
WATER) IN A SAUCEPAN,
SET IT ON A LOW FLAME,
STIR UNTIL THE SUGAR IS
DISSOLVED, AND LET IT
SIMMER FOR 5 MINUTES.
IT DISSOLVES INSTANTLY
IN DRINKS! PLUS YOU CAN
MAKE IT IN A JIFFY AND
STORE IT FOREVER IN THE
FRIDGE.

• FELIX'S TURKEY SHOOT (WILD TURKEY SOUR) •

For 1 drink:
2¼ ounces Wild Turkey
  (preferably 101 proof)
1½ ounces fresh lemon juice
1½ ounces Rose's lime juice
1 teaspoon superfine sugar or 1
  teaspoon simple syrup (see
  sidebar)

For a batch:
1½ cups Wild Turkey
1 cup fresh lemon juice
1 cup Rose's lime juice
2 tablespoons superfine sugar or
  1 ounce simple syrup (see
  sidebar)

Shake over ice in a cocktail shaker; strain into chilled sour glasses. Garnish each with an orange slice.

• MARTINI AU KURANT •

Ever wonder what to do with some of the new wonderfully flavored vodkas? This version of the martini, which takes advantage of Absolut Kurant, is a specialty of the house at Meridiana, a New York City restaurant.

Tiny trickle sweet vermouth   *2 ounces Absolut Kurant*

Shake over ice, and strain into a chilled martini glass. Garnish with an orange twist.

• BLOODY MARY •

1½ ounces vodka
3 ounces tomato juice
Juice of ½ lime
⅛ teaspoon grated fresh
   horseradish, or ½ teaspoon
   prepared

1 dash celery salt
2 dashes Worcestershire sauce

Pour ingredients into an ice-filled cocktail shaker, and shake. Strain over ice into a tall glass. Garnish with a lime.

• WATERMELON MARTINI •

This wonderfully refreshing cocktail, with a kiss of watermelon, is one of the house drinks at Nosmo King, in New York City. Although it's impossible to achieve without a juicer, it's so lovely—especially in the summertime—that I thought I'd include it just in case. If you don't have Absolut Citron, substitute plain vodka plus a squeeze of lemon to achieve the same effect.

For 1 drink:
¼ ounce dry vermouth
2 ounces Absolut Citron vodka
½ ounce fresh watermelon juice

For 4 drinks:
¼ ounce dry vermouth
8 ounces (1 cup) Absolut
*   Citron*
2 ounces fresh watermelon juice

Fill a cocktail shaker with ice. Pour in vermouth to coat ice, and pour out excess. Pour in vodka and watermelon juice, shake, and strain into martini glasses.

VARIATION: GIN WATERMELON MARTINI
Follow the same directions, substituting gin for vodka, and add a splash of lemon.

• JAEBIRD •

Created by Jae Gruenke, a bartender at New York City's Meridiana, who has a particular fondness for Absolut Kurant.

1 ounce Absolut Kurant vodka   *3 ounces soda*
3 ounces pineapple juice

Pour over ice cubes in a tall glass.

• METROPOLITAN •

Another one care of Meridiana in Metropolitan New York City.

1 ounce Absolut Kurant vodka
Splash of Triple Sec

1 ounce cranberry juice
Splash of soda

Pour vodka, Triple Sec, and cranberry juice into an ice-filled shaker. Shake well, and pour into a chilled martini glass. Add a splash of soda, and garnish with a lime.

• DAIQUIRI •

I like my daiquiris tart—for sweeter ones, double the amount of simple syrup.

For 3 drinks:
6 ounces white rum
2 ounces freshly squeezed lime juice

½ ounce simple syrup (see sidebar, page 214)

Rub the rims of cocktail glasses with a cut lime, and dip in superfine sugar. Shake above ingredients over ice and pour into cocktail glasses.

• PINK DAIQUIRI •

For 3 drinks: *½ ounce grenadine*
6 ounces white rum
2 ounces freshly squeezed lime
    juice

Rub the rims of cocktail glasses with a cut lime, and dip in superfine sugar. Shake above ingredients over ice and pour into cocktail glasses.

• PLANTER'S PUNCH •

2 ounces dark rum   *Dash of grenadine*
3 ounces orange juice   *1 teaspoon simple syrup (see*
1 ounce lemon juice   *sidebar, page 214) or superfine*
                               sugar

Shake over ice, and pour into an ice-filled tumbler. Garnish with a slice of orange and a maraschino cherry.

• PIÑA COLADA •

I often find piña coladas way too sweet—which they inevitably are if you use coconut cream rather than coconut milk. You'll love this one—creamy, smooth, island-fruity, and a little sweet.

2 ounces light rum   *4 ounces pineapple juice*
2 ounces coconut milk*

Shake vigorously over ice in a cocktail shaker; strain into goblets. Garnish with a pineapple spear.

• MAI TAI •

"Anybody who says I didn't create this drink is a dirty stinker," wrote Victor Bergeron, alias Trader Vic. Bergeron invented this drink in 1944, at his restaurant in Oakland, California. He gave the first two to two friends of his from Tahiti, one of whom tasted it and said, "Mai Tai, Roa Aé," which means "Out of this world—the best." The original creation calls for shaved ice, but since that's a little hard to swing at a cocktail party, I've altered it slightly.

Juice of ½ lime (about ½   *½ ounce orgeat, or other*
*   ounce)*   *   almond syrup*
1 ounce light rum   *½ ounce Curaçao, or other*
1 ounce dark rum   *   orange liqueur*

Shake over plenty of ice in a cocktail shaker; strain into ice-filled old-fashioned glass. Garnish with the empty lime shell and a healthy sprig of mint.

*Available in the imported foods section of many supermarkets.

• HAPPY DAVE •

1½ ounces Mount Gay rum
4½ ounces Ocean Spray guava
     drink

2 dashes grenadine

Pour Mount Gay rum and guava drink into an ice-filled cocktail shaker and shake. Strain over ice into an old-fashioned glass, garnish with a squeeze of lime, stir, then add 2 dashes of grenadine.

• BOMPI'S PUNCH •

1 ounce light rum
1 ounce dark rum
½ ounce Cointreau
1½ ounces orange juice

1½ ounces pineapple juice
½ ounce fresh lime juice
4 dashes grenadine

Shake over ice in a cocktail shaker. Strain into an ice-filled old-fashioned glass. Garnish with a pineapple wedge, maraschino cherry, and an umbrella.

• GUY'S BLUE HAWAII •

For 1 drink:
1½ ounces white rum
¾ ounce blue Curaçao
2 ounces pineapple juice
1 ounce cream of coconut

For 6 drinks:
1 cup white rum
½ cup blue Curaçao
1½ cups pineapple juice
¾ cup cream of coconut

Shake over ice in a cocktail shaker; strain into ice-filled goblets. Garnish with an umbrella, a slice of pineapple, and a maraschino cherry.

• CUBA LIBRE •

I always used to think of this drink as "Rum and Coke," and therefore sickeningly sweet. It's not! It's light, refreshing, and altogether charming!

Juice of ½ lime
1 ounce light rum

Cola

Pour lime juice over ice in an old-fashioned glass. Drop in rind from the lime. Pour in rum, and fill with cola. Garnish with lime.

• COGNAC MARTINI •

2 ounces cognac   *½ teaspoon fresh lemon juice*

Fill a martini pitcher with ice, add cognac and lemon juice, stir, and strain into a martini glass. Garnish with a lemon twist.

• SIDECAR •

1 ounce cognac   *½ ounce freshly squeezed lemon*
½ ounce Cointreau   *juice*

Shake over ice, and strain into a martini glass. Garnish with a twist.

• FRENCH 75 •

This drink, which dates back to World War I, was invented by American doughboys bivouacked in Champagne, France.

1 sugar cube   *champagne*
1½ ounces cognac

Place the sugar cube in a champagne flute; add cognac. Fill with champagne (about 2½ ounces), and garnish with a twist.

FRENCH 75

• CAIPIRINHA •

Cachaça, the popular sugarcane liquor of Brazil, or *aguá ardente de cana* is the basis of many tangy cocktails. Blanca Fulô is one brand that's imported by the U.S., but others, such as Janeiro, can also be turned up. If you like the Caipirinha, do as the Brazilians do and invent variations using other fruit juices—mango, orange, pineapple, coconut milk, passion fruit, etc. If you add a raw egg white (1 for 6 drinks), it becomes a *batida.*

For 6 drinks:
8 ounces cachaça
Juice of 4 limes

2 heaping tablespoons sugar
Lime slices for garnish

Dissolve sugar in the lime juice in a shaker. Add cachaça, shake, pour into glasses with ice, and garnish with lime slices.

• BAHIA •

1½ ounces cachaça
1 ounce Triple Sec

2 ounces orange-pineapple juice

Shake over ice in a cocktail shaker. Strain over ice into an old-fashioned glass, and garnish with a squeeze of lime.

• COCO-LIME BATIDA •

1½ ounces cachaça
Juice of ½ lime
2 ounces coconut milk

½ ounce egg white
½ ounces simple syrup (see sidebar, page 214)

Shake vigorously over plenty of ice in a cocktail shaker until frothy. Strain into a cocktail glass. Garnish with a few shreds of coconut on top.

• CHAMPAGNE COCKTAIL •

You needn't use an expensive champagne; try the sparkling whites from California made by French champagne makers— Domaine Carneros and Domaine Chandon both make excellent affordable bruts.

4 ounces champagne or brut sparkling white wine
1 sugar cube

2 dashes bitters

Place the sugar cube in the bottom of a champagne flute. Sprinkle with bitters, and fill glass with champagne. Garnish with a lemon peel knot. *(Note:* 1 bottle makes 6 cocktails.)

• NEGRONI •

1 ounce Campari   1 ounce red vermouth
1 ounce gin

Fill a cocktail shaker with ice, add ingredients, and shake
well. Strain into a chilled martini glass, and garnish with a
twist.

• LONGEY •

This was created by Rick Long, the bartender at Man Ray in
New York, who calls it "a great summertime drink."

1 ounce Myers's rum   1½ ounces orange juice
½ ounce Mount Gay rum   ½ ounce cranberry juice
½ ounce Campari   Dash of grenadine
½ ounce Cointreau

Shake over ice in a cocktail shaker. Strain into a martini
glass, and garnish with a lemon and lime twist.

• AURORA BOREALIS •

I invented this drink to go with Gravlax Canapés at the last cocktail party I had—and every single guest ordered *at least* one!

1 ounce Aquavit   *½ ounce blueberry syrup*
3 ounces grapefruit juice

Pour into an ice-filled cocktail shaker, and shake well. Strain over ice into an old-fashioned glass, and garnish with three blueberries threaded onto a cocktail toothpick with a frilly hat.

• MARGARITA •

1½ ounces tequila   *Juice of ½ lime*
½ ounce Triple Sec

Rub the rim of a goblet or old-fashioned glass with the cut side of a lime, then dip rim into a plate of salt. Fill with ice. Pour ingredients over ice into a cocktail shaker, and shake well. Strain into glass. Garnish with a slice of lime.

• VERMOUTH CASSIS •

2 ounces dry vermouth   *½ ounce crème de cassis*

Pour over ice in an old-fashioned glass, and stir. Garnish with a twist.

• BIANCO •

My house summertime aperitif.

3 ounces Cinzano Bianco   *Splash of soda*
  (sweet white vermouth)

Pour Cinzano Bianco over ice in an old-fashioned glass, add a splash of soda, and stir. Garnish with a squeeze of lemon.

• CIN-CIN •

This delightful aperitif comes from the back of the Cinzano bottle.

2 ounces Cinzano Rosso (sweet   *2 ounces Cinzano Dry (dry*
  red vermouth)   *white vermouth)*

Pour into an old-fashioned glass, over ice. Stir, and garnish with a twist.

• CAMPARI AND TONIC •

1½ ounces Campari   4 ounces tonic water

Pour Campari into an ice-filled old-fashioned glass, add tonic water, and stir. Garnish with a slice of lime.

• CAMPARI AND ORANGE JUICE •

1 ounce Campari   3 ounces orange juice

Pour into an ice-filled old-fashioned glass and stir.

• KIR ROYALE •

3½ ounces champagne or brut   ½ ounce cassis
   sparkling white wine from
   California, such as
   Domaine Carneros or
   Domaine Chandon

Pour champagne into a champagne flute, and add cassis. Garnish with a twist.

• KIR ROYALE MAISON •

3½ ounces champagne or brut sparkling white wine from California, such as Domaine Carneros or Domaine Chandon

½ ounce blackberry syrup, or any other fruit syrup you love

Pour champagne into a flute, and add fruit syrup. Garnish with a knot of lemon peel.

• PEACH BELLINI •

Use the ripest summer peaches you can find; peel and puree them in a food processor or blender.

For 8 Bellinis:
1½ cups pureed fresh peaches

1 bottle champagne or brut sparkling white wine from California, such as Domaine Carneros or Domaine Chandon

Pour champagne flutes ⅓ full of peach puree; fill to top with champagne.

THE ALCOHOL-FREE ZONE

• SHIRLEY TEMPLE •

6 ounces ginger ale   *3 dashes grenadine*

Pour well-chilled ginger ale into a martini glass; add grenadine. Garnish with a lemon peel knot, or a slice of lime and a maraschino cherry.

• LEMON TWIST •

6 ounces lemonade   *Generous splash of soda*
Dash blackberry syrup (or any
    other berry syrup, or
    grenadine)

Fill cocktail shaker with ice, pour in lemonade and blackberry syrup, and shake well. Pour over ice into tall glass, and add splash of soda. Garnish with a twist.

• WATER COCKTAIL •

Experiment with this one, using your own favorite brands!

*2 ounces Evian, or New York
   City tap water*

*2 ounces San Pellegrino water
2 ounces Perrier*

Pour Evian or New York City tap water into ice-filled cocktail shaker; shake well, and strain into champagne flute. Add
sparkling waters, and garnish with a lemon peel knot.

• CLASSIC WATER COCKTAIL •

*Note: not strictly alcohol-free, just very low in alcohol, as bitters
contain alcohol.*

*Sugar cube
3 dashes bitters*

*Sparkling mineral water or
   club soda*

Place sugar cube in the bottom of an old-fashioned glass, and
sprinkle with bitters. Add 2 or 3 ice cubes, and fill with
sparkling mineral water or club soda. Garnish with a maraschino cherry and a squeeze of lemon.

231

• FLAVORED MINERAL WATER •

5 ounces San Pellegrino,
    Perrier, or other sparkling
    mineral water

½ ounce blackberry, blueberry,
    raspberry, red currant, or
    other fruit syrup

Pour over 2 or 3 ice cubes in an old-fashioned glass; garnish
with a squeeze of lime.

• ORANGE FLOWER •

Sugar cube
3 dashes orange flower water

San Pellegrino water, well
    chilled

Place sugar cube in bottom of a champagne flute, and sprinkle with orange flower water. Add a few drops of San
Pellegrino water, and muddle. Fill glass with San Pellegrino
water, and garnish with an orange peel knot.

• VIRGIN DAVE •

6 ounces Ocean Spray guava
    drink
Splash club soda

3 dashes grenadine

Pour guava drink over ice in an old-fashioned glass. Add a splash of club soda, and a squeeze of lime, and stir. Add grenadine last; garnish with a lime slice, a maraschino cherry, and an umbrella.

• BLUE TAHITI •

This may not *look* blue, but it *tastes* blue, and very tropical.

3 ounces pineapple juice
3 ounces coconut milk

1 ounce blueberry syrup

Shake vigorously over ice in a cocktail shaker; strain into a goblet. Garnish with a pineapple spear, a maraschino cherry, and an umbrella.

• AMERICAN GOTHIC •

If you don't already have a juicer, this fabulous vegetable juice blend may persuade you to get one. It's especially great in the cooler months, when fruit drinks seem out of season at a cocktail party.

2 tomatoes
3 carrots
3 stalks celery

1 cucumber
1 handful parsley, including
   stems
1 red pepper

233

Put all the vegetables through a juicer. Salt to taste, if desired. Serve in a chilled martini glass, garnished with an olive.

MAKES 28 OUNCES, ENOUGH FOR 4 OR 5 DRINKS.

• AMERICAN "COCKTAIL" •

*4 ounces American Gothic
  vegetable juice*
3 dashes Worcestershire sauce

3 dashes Tabasco sauce
Salt to taste

TO MAKE GINGER JUICE:
PEEL A PIECE OF GINGER
ROOT, AND GRATE IT
FINELY. WRAP THE GRATED
GINGER IN A SMALL PIECE
OF CHEESECLOTH, AND
SQUEEZE IT OVER A GLASS
UNTIL LIQUID DRIBBLES
OUT. VOILÀ—FRESH
GINGER JUICE!

Shake in an ice-filled cocktail shaker, and strain into an ice-filled old-fashioned glass. Garnish with a squeeze of lemon.

• WINTER SPECIAL •

Another one for the juicer—this is the most delicious drink in the world. For an easy way to make the ginger juice, see the sidebar.

3 ounces carrot juice
1 ounce beet juice
¼ teaspoon ginger juice

Stir in a pitcher to combine; pour into a champagne flute or sherry glass.

• BUGS •

Hurray! You can make this one without a juicer, since freshly squeezed carrot juice is widely available in health food stores and many supermarkets.

3 ounces carrot juice   *¼ teaspoon ginger juice*
1½ ounces orange juice

Pour over two ice cubes in an old-fashioned glass; garnish with a sprig of mint.

• CREAMY COCO-CARROT •

2 ounces carrot juice   *2 ounces coconut milk*

Shake over ice in a cocktail shaker; strain into a champagne flute.

• VIRGIN MARY •

5 ounces tomato juice   *1 dash celery salt*
Juice of ½ lime   *2 dashes Worcestershire sauce*
*⅛ teaspoon grated fresh
    horseradish, or ½ teaspoon
    prepared*

235

Pour ingredients into an ice-filled cocktail shaker, and shake. Strain over ice into a tall glass. Garnish with a lime.

• VIRGIN GIN & TONIC •

8 ounces tonic water

Pour over ice into a tall glass; garnish with a squeeze of lime.

• VIRGIN VODKA & TONIC •

8 ounces tonic water

Pour over ice into a tall glass; garnish with a squeeze of lime.

• BITTER ORANGE •

This tastes like a virgin Campari Orange.

1½ ounces Pellegrino "Bitter"   *4 ounces orange juice*

Pour over rocks in an old-fashioned glass.

7

AT THE PARTY

Here's a problem I'll bet you haven't thought of (just what you want to hear right when people are about to walk in!). It's a potential mistake made by many a rookie host, but since you're reading this *ahead* of time, it can't possibly happen to you. A good thing, too, because a sticky problem it is: What to do about the telephone?

After all, you haven't invited everyone you know, and if someone calls who wasn't invited, you don't want them to hear a cocktail party going on (ice clinking in glasses, animated chatter, etc.). It could be traumatic, not to mention insulting. The mistake that many hosts make is neglecting to ponder this issue until just before the doorbell is about to ring for the first time. No problem, you say to yourself, we'll just leave the answering machine on. Okay, Smarty-pants, but what happens if someone is calling to say that they're lost? Keep the volume up and screen the calls, you say? Isn't that kind of *obnoxious*? Of course it is! So what does the cocktail party expert suggest? A compromise, which I'm sure you'll find unsatisfactory somehow, but here it is: answer your phone only up until the first guest arrives. If the caller is someone who isn't invited, make an excuse and get off the phone quickly. After the first guest walks in, and before many others arrive, turn off the ringer on the phone, turn down the volume on the machine, and if you hear it click on, turn it up for a second to hear who's calling. If it's someone you're expecting, pick it up; if not, turn it down again, and let 'em chatter away all night long if they want to. Once everyone you're expecting has arrived, don't even think about answering it again.

DO MINGLE.

(

With that bugbear out of the way, let's turn our by now probably overtaxed attention to the subject of

YOUR   RESPONSIBILITIES
AS   HOST

Your most important job as host is to make your guests feel comfortable. Sure, that means that you must attend to their needs. But don't fall into the trap of thinking that if everything about your cocktail party isn't absolutely perfect, it's the end of the world. It isn't! If you're so wrapped up in trying to make sure everything is *perfect* that you become a miserable wreck, your guests will surely take note, and become miserable themselves. Hence,

"A WOEFUL HOSTESS BROOKS NOT MERRY GUESTS."
—SHAKESPEARE, THE RAPE OF LUCRECE

> RULE #9: RELAX. IF YOU'RE MISERABLE,
> YOUR GUESTS WILL BE TOO.

That's why before they cross the threshold at the appointed hour, it's very important to sit down quietly for a moment, relax, gather all your charm and good grace, and repeat the following cocktail party mantra:

I'm doing this because I want to.
I'm doing this because I want to.
I'm doing this because I want to.

Feel better? Good. Oh—now what is that? I think I hear the doorbell!

Unlike the parties we had when we were callow youths, when a 9:00 P.M. start time meant no one came until 10:00 or 10:30, people do arrive at cocktail parties on time. First of all, if it's a weekday, many will be coming directly from work, and even if they habitually work later than 6:00, your cocktail party will provide them with a handy excuse to leave the office early. Second of all, if everyone showed up an hour late to a cocktail party, they'd miss half of it, and therefore half of the hors d'oeuvres. Thirdly, and most significantly, "fashionably late" loses all its fashionability when it comes to a cocktail party.

Therefore, for a cocktail party called for 6:00 P.M., you

☾

can expect most everyone to arrive between 6:00 and 6:20. If someone asks you what time they *really* should arrive, simply tell them the party will *really* begin at six, and *really* end at eight, and they may come whenever they like.

Since it begins promptly, be sure to be completely dressed. This may sound obvious, but it's amazing how many hosts will leave showering and getting dressed to the very last minute. If you do this when you're having a cocktail party, and a guest whose watch is running fast walks in five minutes before the starting time, you risk answering the door before you've had time to put on your shoes, or answering the door with shaving cream on your face, or without having applied your lipstick.

As soon as you take the coats of the first arrivals, offer them a drink, and then put the first hot hors d'oeuvres to be heated in the oven. In *that* order. This way, by the time you have six or eight people, a batch will come out. In the meantime, you may pass a tray of canapés or cold hors d'oeuvres, plus you might have a bowl or two of spiced nuts or somesuch; if the crowd stays very thin for some time, you may refresh the tray as more guests arrive.

At the start of the party, when there are only a few guests, you should introduce them, if they aren't already introduced. If you can think of something they have in common or someone they know in common, you might mention it right off the bat, so they immediately have something to talk about. As more guests arrive, continue introducing them until the number of guests makes doing so cumbersome (which will happen rather soon), at which point they will go ahead and introduce themselves. If you say something like, "Please go ahead and introduce yourselves while I get some hors d'oeuvres," then no one will be miffed.

As the party gets under way, think about the timing of the hors d'oeuvres. If they are as delicious as they ought to be, they will be snapped up very quickly. If you overload the trays, you will give a false sense of bounty—this isn't intended to be dinner, yet don't forget that your guests haven't eaten since lunch. The key, then, is *pace*.

This is especially true for delicacies such as chilled shrimp. It can be a remarkable thing to behold that adults with usually impeccable manners can suddenly appear as though they haven't eaten for a week when a platter of chilled shrimp and tangy cocktail sauce sails up to them. So do yourself and the later-arriving guests a favor and plan to pass the shrimp at least three or four times—you may even want to divide it up beforehand.

DIVISION OF LABOR

Although a small cocktail party (up to fifteen guests or so) may be handled effectively by one host, mixing drinks, passing hors d'oeuvres, answering the door, and changing the CD, it's much more easily handled by a couple. So enlist the help of your spouse or boyfriend or girlfriend, and divide the duties. If you don't have a significant other, ask a friend to be a hero and help.

I suggest one person be responsible for bartending, going to the freezer for more ice, getting more chilled bottles

DO NOT PUT OUT
CIGARETTES IN A
HOUSEPLANT.

out of the fridge as needed, and changing the CD when necessary. The other should be responsible for passing hors d'oeuvres, noticing whether anyone needs his or her drink refreshed, refilling the hors d'oeuvre trays in the kitchen, and answering the door.

You may decide to let guests mix their own drinks, but if you do, it should be obvious what needs to go in them, or someone should be handy nearby to make sure guests know what to do. But this option isn't recommended, since the idea is for guests to feel taken care of.

If you have done all the work of planning the party without your significant other's help, you'll have to have a ten-minute coaching session beforehand. If you're delegating the bartending duties, you'll have to remind him or her how to mix whatever drinks you've chosen, and stress the importance of the proper garnish. (Of course everything will be right there on the bar already, and the garnishes already cut and prepared.) Don't forget to show your bartender which glasses are for which drinks.

If your significant other is doing hors d'oeuvre duty, you'll have to show him or her how many trays you have prepared, and discuss pace. The trays should be passed once, and then left in a convenient spot. The remaining finger food may disappear off it right away, in which case remove the tray to the kitchen, but *do not* bring out more hors d'oeuvres until you are ready to.

Also, remind him or her to notice people's drinks, and offer them another if necessary.

OFFERING DRINKS

And while we're on the subject, if a guest refuses a cocktail, immediately offer an alcohol-free drink, making that drink sound as appealing as possible. *Do not* try to convince him or her to have a cocktail. This is an especially important point, as the guest may be involved in a twelve-step program, in which case being at a cocktail party may not be the easiest thing in the world for him or her.

You should also know that it is your responsibility to ensure that a guest doesn't leave your home drunk and get behind the wheel of an automobile. Besides the fact that you care about the safety of that guest and others on the road, you may also be legally liable if an accident should happen. In a place such as New York City, where people tend to use public transportation rather than drive, this probably won't be an issue. But when you do know that a guest has driven to the party, and that guest is getting visibly drunk, do not offer another cocktail. Instead, try to get them to have an alcohol-free drink. This is tricky, though, because you don't want to be preachy. You might have, say, a Shirley Temple yourself, and remark how delicious and refreshing it is.

What's likely to happen, though, is that many guests will alternate between a cocktail or two, and then a soda or another alcohol-free drink, especially as the party wears on.

It *is* the host's responsibility to keep the glasses filled with *something,* though, so do be vigilant.

AIDING IN MINGLING

It is also your responsibility to make sure no one is off by himself with no one to talk to. If you should spot such a guest, go talk to him yourself for a bit, and while you're doing so, think of someone he has something in common with, and introduce the two. If the other person is already involved in a conversation, wait until there is a break in it, then introduce your wallflower into the group.

Do not let your guests feel that they've been invited out of a sense of obligation on your part, or that you would feel guilty if you didn't invite them. Even if it's true. Let's face it: sometimes there will be people whom you're maybe not crazy about, but who have invited *you* many times, or people whom you're not crazy about but their best friend is invited and they're sure to hear about it and feel badly if they're not invited; or people whom you *are* perhaps crazy about, but you can't invite them without their spouses, whom you *can't* stand.

And then there are those you have invited because you find them somehow *useful,* as in the brilliant, charming conversationalist, single men when there are a surfeit of single women, or people you think will impress other guests.

Okay—maybe it's true—we often have ulterior motives that we're not proud of for inviting certain guests. Yet in *none* of these cases must these guests be allowed to think anything other than that they have been invited because you want them to be there! Therefore, as the host, you should try to

chat *at least for a moment* with each of your guests; do not ig-
nore anyone. Of course, if you have forty people, this will be
much more difficult to achieve than if you have fifteen. But
with forty, your guests will understand that you cannot be in
forty places at one time.

It is also your job, as much as possible, to try to smooth
over any conflicts arising between your guests. You'd be
amazed at the kinds of mini-maelstroms that can stir themselves up in a party lasting only two hours! Therefore, if you
see two people getting into an overly heated argument,
breeze up to them and change the subject. As host, this is
easy to do, since the social rules regulating cocktail party behavior allow the host different behavior than they do the
guests. Whereas a guest would never walk into a conversation
and change the subject outright, a host can walk up and say
anything related to the mechanics of the party: Can I get
anyone a drink? Is everyone okay? You can even walk up to
the group with another new guest in tow and say, Have you
met so-and-so? If you employ this tactic, pretend not to notice that there was an argument, so as not to embarrass the
two arguers. Then you can either continue talking to them,
employing of course a new mode of more *friendly* conversation, or you can apologize for the interruption, and go refresh
their drinks. In most cases, at this point they would feel silly
resuming the argument.

PARTY ETIQUETTE: A GUIDE FOR GUESTS AND HOSTS

DO ASK FOR AN RSVP. BUT WHATEVER YOU DO, DON'T SAY "PLEASE RSVP." SINCE RSVP IS FRENCH FOR "RÉPONDEZ S'IL VOUS PLAIT," OR "RESPOND, PLEASE," SAYING "PLEASE RSVP" IS LIKE SAYING "PLEASE RESPOND PLEASE."

☾

A cocktail party is the most social of social occasions, drawing on everyone's manners and social skills to make it a smashing success. As such, there are certain *rules* that must be followed—by host and guest alike. Furthermore, anyone reading this book, and therefore thinking about throwing a cocktail party, will no doubt be invited to other cocktail parties as a guest, so it seems advisable that the host should also know how to be a good guest.

RESPONDING TO AN INVITATION

Let's back up to what happens *before* the party, and talk for a moment about responding to the invitation. Guests must take RSVPs seriously. If it weren't important for the host to know, why would he ask? First of all, he has to figure out how many hors d'oeuvres and drinks will be required, according to a formula, and he'll have to make purchases accordingly. He certainly mustn't be caught short by someone who didn't respond to the invitation and then shows up unexpectedly.

On the other hand, and this is what no-show guests fail to consider—the hosts don't want to plan for more than will actually attend. If they buy too much liquor, they may be able to return it for a refund, but if they prepare too many hors d'oeuvres, they'll go to waste, which is a cocktail party sin. They can't simply serve the extras if there are people they planned for who didn't show up because then the guests won't be hungry for dinner, and they'll never leave.

So do respond, and as quickly as possible after the invitation is extended. If an illness or emergency arises, of course your hosts will understand, but if you and ten other guests choose not to appear because you're tired or not in the mood, they may resent the unnecessary monetary outlay and waste, and with just cause. If you responded yes, that you would come, and then find you cannot make it, call *as soon as possible* in advance—so maybe the food won't yet have been bought.

"BE NOT FORGETFUL TO ENTERTAIN STRANGERS, FOR THEREBY SOME HAVE ENTERTAINED ANGELS UNAWARES."
—HEBREWS 13:2

☾

BRINGING EXTRA GUESTS

When an invitation is extended to someone who is known to have a significant other, it should be understood that the invitation includes both. When you respond, however, say something like "Y and I would love to be there," or "I'd love to come, but unfortunately, Z will be out of town," so your host knows whether to expect one or two of you.

If you want to bring someone *other* than your regular squeeze, i.e., a date, or a friend, or a business acquaintance whom your host might enjoy meeting, it is up to you to ask your host if this is okay. That being the case, do make sure that person can actually come, so as not to put your host in

DO ARRIVE EMPTY-
HANDED. (THIS IS NOT A
DINNER PARTY.)

☾

the position of providing for another person, which involves extra money and work—and then not having her show up.

And what if you suddenly, out of the blue, find yourself with an out-of-town visitor on your doorstep—can you bring him at the last minute? The answer is to call ahead—it's very possible a few people have gotten sick or whatever, so the host may indeed welcome your guest as a replacement.

MAKING AN ENTRANCE

The best time to arrive at a cocktail party is five to twenty minutes after the start. It's okay to walk in punctually, but at the same time it might be nice to give your host a chance to sit down and catch his breath for a moment. And remember, fashionably late to a cocktail party is unfashionable.

HOW TO DRESS

Women should show up in a cocktail dress. This is basically any festive dress that is above the knee. Décolletage is acceptable, as is wearing a very short dress, if fashion so dictates. Shoes should have a little lift to the heel, probably a pump or mule of some sort, or strappy sandals in the summer. The reasons for what sounds like a rather strict dress code are twofold. The first is *tradition.* The good guest wants to reaffirm the *idea* of the cocktail party. (As we read in Chapter 1, the cocktail dress is on the Top Ten List of Cocktail Party Signifiers.) The second reason, which is related, is that by wearing a cocktail dress, she is acknowledging the fact that there are certain things which make a cocktail party a cocktail party, and she is letting her hosts know that she's aware they have gone through a great deal of time and expense to put the whole thing together, even if by showtime it will appear effortless. In this way, the cocktail dress is a badge of *respect* for the host.

For the men, there is no rigid code of dress, but it's nice to wear an ironed shirt that doesn't have too many stains on it, and to have shaved at least that morning. Remember that many people will be wearing business attire, however (unless you run in a crowd of "creative" types or your friends work with their hands. . . .), so dress, if not elegantly, then with a certain level of élan.

Guests do not need to come bearing gifts. This may be difficult for those who wouldn't dream of showing up at a dinner party without at least a bottle of wine. But think of it this way: The cocktail party is not a dinner party. (See Rule Number One.) You're not getting dinner, so you don't *need* to supply wine.

Do not arrive with flowers. Even if your host adores them as a rule, when ten people are coming in the door at one time, the last thing he wants to do is rummage around for a vase. If you are one of those people for whom it is impossible not to bring something, offer the hosts a bottle of something interesting, or chocolates, or a CD—something to which they can say, "Oh, how thoughtful," and put it down and forget about it until later. In this case, do not draw attention to the gift; you don't want to embarrass anyone who enters empty-handed, which most people will.

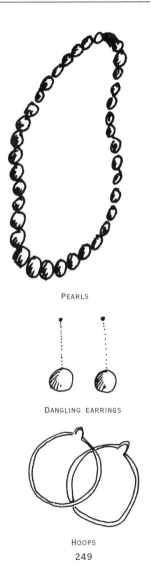

PEARLS

DANGLING EARRINGS

HOOPS

249

If, again, you feel you simply must offer a gift—for instance if the party is being given in your honor—and you really really *really* want to be classy, *send* your hosts a flower arrangement earlier in the day. This way, they'll have time to use it as part of the decor for the party, and it will be seen, rather than as a pleasant nuisance, as a lovely and thoughtful gift.

MINGLING AND CONVERSING

Since it *is* a social occasion, the guests must mingle. Did the hairs just rise on your neck? Do you *hate* mingling? Well, you'll simply have to learn how.

Just as many more people than one would suspect consider themselves shy, there are multitudes out there in the world who do not like to attend cocktail parties simply because they think they don't know how to mingle. But it's really very simple, and anyone who follows these tips will surely find himself more than comfortable at cocktail parties.

First off, one needn't be frightened or anxious. Try to remember that there are more people like you who think they don't know how to mingle than people who are comfortable with it.

COCKTAIL DRESS, SHOWN MINGLING

I used to be one of those people who were afraid of mingling. But since I moved to New York City in my midtwenties, and hardly knew anyone, I knew that I had *better* mingle, and fast. I discovered that if I was invited to a cocktail party where I wasn't likely to know anyone, I should go *by myself.* In this way, I was forced to talk to people I didn't know, because *not* to do so would be to stand forlornly by myself, or else have a canapé and slink out the door, which I was not about to do.

I also discovered very quickly that the worst possible strategy is to go with a friend, for you end up talking to your friend the whole time, since this is the only person you know, and therefore it's impossible to meet anyone new. In fact, I recently learned that one married couple I know used to arrive at a cocktail party and pretend that they didn't know each other, so that they could more effectively mingle! While I think that's going a little too far, I do think it's good for couples not to stick together like glue all evening, so they can mix a little.

The strategy of going by oneself is also one familiar to people who are single—they know it's much easier to be gregarious and social if one's buddy isn't stapled to one's bosom.

Okay, so you're by yourself, you don't know anyone, you feel a little awkward. *How exactly do you mingle?*

The first thing one must do is start up a conversation. This is really not so very difficult as it may seem. You can start one at the bar—making some comment about the drink; this is just as easily achieved as hors d'oeuvres are being passed. When a tray of hors d'oeuvres makes its appearance, people tend to flock around it, so that's a perfect excuse to talk to one of those people, saying something like "Did you have any idea X was such a fabulous cook?" Which can always lead to "How did you meet him or her?" or "Do you cook, yourself? . . . What do you like to make?" etc.

In fact, a useful general rule of conversation is ask a lot

"CANDY

IS DANDY

BUT LIQUOR

IS QUICKER."

—OGDEN NASH, REFLECTION ON ICE-BREAKING

"GOOD BREEDING

CONSISTS IN CONCEALING

HOW MUCH WE THINK OF

OURSELVES AND HOW

LITTLE WE THINK OF THE

OTHER PERSON."

—MARK TWAIN, NOTEBOOKS

☾

of questions. That way the conversation not only keeps going, but the person to whom you're talking has the sense that you're interested in her. And *everyone* likes to feel that way. But the other half of being a good conversationalist is listening to the answers. If you ask something, and think about your next question while the other person is answering, you'll come off as insincere (which you will be), and eventually you'll start to feel like an unsalaried talk-show host. Unless the person you've approached is a total doof or narcissist, he'll eventually start asking you things, too, and before you know it, it will turn into a genuine dialogue.

And what if you espy someone across the room you've been dying to meet? I say, march right up to the person and say, "Hello, I'm so and so—I've been dying to meet you." This approach comes off much better if the comment isn't dripping with sexual innuendo. If it is indeed sincere, the person will probably be flattered and happy to talk to you.

The beauty part of all of the above strategies is that the odds are you'll only have to employ them once. Once you start chatting with one person, someone else is likely to walk up and be introduced, and you'll take off from there.

Certain topics will be taboo for conversation, though not many. It may be cliché for me to recommend avoiding talk of politics and religion, but there's a reason: these are the topics that get people all hot and bothered, and cocktail party talk is supposed to be friendly chatter. This doesn't mean it has to be empty and meaningless, either; you should really *talk* to your conversation partner.

Which doesn't preclude a good argument. But this is

tricky—on the one hand, honest-to-God arguing, as in laying forth an argument, provides some of the most scintillating conversation, but it only works as long as both parties are on the up-and-up, and no one's ego is on the line—there's nothing more boring than someone who always insists on being right. Nor should one simply argue for arguing's sake—the perennial "devil's advocate" comes in a close second to the Know-It-All in the Boring Competition.

TELLING JOKES

Some people try to inject life into party chatter by telling jokes. Usually, though, jokes are *not funny.* Think of the truly funny people you know—do they tell *jokes*? Or do they just say funny things? Odds are, they simply possess an inner funniness, and don't resort to telling jokes.

But if tell jokes you must, follow these simple rules for optimum success. First, always tell them in the present tense: it's funnier. Second, start out with "It seems . . ." (As in "It seems this traveling salesman . . ." I learned this trick by watching *I Love Lucy*). And third, gesticulate a lot— sometimes hand movements are funny all by themselves!

DITCHING A BORE

Sometimes the problem may be not how to start a conversation, or how to conduct one, but rather how to *end* one. For instance, you're stuck talking to a bore, and there's an attractive member of the opposite sex or a charming business connection on the other side of the room.

This can prove to be a sticky situation, yet there are some excellent solutions, a few of which may even be achieved without hurting anyone's feelings.

My favorite is to finish one's drink, and say, simply, "Well, it looks like I need another drink—may I get you one?" This works whether the person says yes or no. If they say no, simply say either "Very nice talking to you," or if that sounds too bleak, try "I'll be back." You won't be, unless you're a masochist, until it's time to say good-bye, if you feel like doing that. If the bore says yes, he or she would like a drink, you make your way across the room (and don't let the bore follow you), get yourself and the bore a drink, but manage to stop for a chat with someone else along the way, then deliver the drink to the bore while gracefully making it clear that you're suddenly involved in a new conversation from which you simply cannot extricate yourself. It's less tricky than it sounds, and a ploy well worth learning if you're the kind of person whom everyone considers a "good listener." (It's a wonderful quality, mind you, but it can be deadly at a cocktail party if you want to talk to more than one person.)

DO PROVIDE PLENTY OF ASHTRAYS IF YOU'RE ALLOWING SMOKING.

DO SHOW GUESTS WHERE THEY MAY SMOKE OUTSIDE IF NOT.

FLIRTING

Flirting is not only acceptable at a cocktail party, it's encouraged. (Unless of course you're married or otherwise committed and your significant other will be offended.) But it *is* possible to flirt innocently. One way is to somehow flatter the person you're talking to. Flattery may get you nowhere, but maybe you don't want to *go* anywhere, you just want to flirt. All flirting really means is being charming and attentive to the person you're talking to—though not to the exclusion of other guests. The one exception is that you should not flirt with a single person if you happen to know that a friend of yours present has a crush on that person—but that's just plain human decency! If you do decide to go into a flirtatious mode, do it democratically, do it morally, and then go ahead and flirt shamelessly.

SMOKING

If you must smoke, and no one else is doing so, it may very well be that your host doesn't like cigarette smoke! First look to see if there are ashtrays lying around—if there aren't, you'll probably have to go outside or go home or even refrain from smoking. If there *are* ashtrays, you may be in luck. Either way, politeness dictates that you must ask your host. Do not simply light up. If you ask the host, and it does seem to be okay, try not to blow smoke directly into the faces of other guests, who may not appreciate it. Try to stand near an open window, if possible. Do not put out your cigarette in a houseplant or a highball glass, nor grind it into the carpet. Find an ashtray. This may sound elementary, yet it's amazing how many guests with otherwise meticulous manners suddenly forget them when it comes to disposing of cigarettes.

And what of smoking marijuana? Decidedly not at a cocktail party, if only for the simple reason that if you start

DO NOT PUT OUT YOUR CIGARETTE IN A HIGHBALL GLASS.

255

WHAT DO YOU DO WITH

THE TOOTHPICK AFTER YOU

USE IT?

"IF A TOOTHPICK IS USED

TO SPEAR THE FOOD, IT

SHOULD BE PLACED IN A

RECEPTACLE PUT OUT FOR

THAT PURPOSE, IN AN

ASHTRAY, OR IN ONE'S

NAPKIN—NOT BACK ON

THE SERVING TRAY, OR IN

THE NEAREST POTTED

PLANT."

—CRAIG CLAIBORNE,

ELEMENTS OF ETIQUETTE

passing reefers, you and the other guests will get too hungry, and throw off the host's meticulously calculated hors d'oeuvre count, and you'll have to go off and have dinner before the party's halfway through.

OFFERING TO HELP

Offering to help is thoughtful, though completely unnecessary at a cocktail party. The host wants you there to relax and enjoy yourself, and knows that it is her time to work.

If help you must, though, it's nice to offer to spell the bartender. If you do this, do not decide that your recipe for a Manhattan is much better than the house's—if you want to *help,* ask the bartender to tell you the recipes.

The other option is to offer to pass hors d'oeuvres for a while, or to help with last-minute garnishings as trays come out of the fridge.

EATING AND DRINKING

Probably the burning question you've been dying to ask is: "Is it okay if I reuse a toothpick after eating one hors d'oeuvre—say a chilled shrimp—off of it?"

The answer is *yes.* As long as you take the first morsel you touch with the reused toothpick.

On the other hand, it's *not* okay to dip an hors d'oeuvre in a sauce more than once—otherwise, you'll be putting the "cooties" from your first bite into the entire dish of sauce.

And what if god forbid you *spill* something on the

white carpet? Nonchalantly clean it up. Ask the bartending host for a little club soda, pour it on the spot, and find a clean cloth in the kitchen to blot it with. Don't rub, don't use a colored paper napkin (the dye might run), and don't make a big deal out of it.

As for cocktails, drink them in moderation—after all, the goal isn't to get drunk; it's to socialize. Ask for something alcohol-free in between cocktails. Nevertheless, if you came in a car, it's a good idea to have a designated driver.

"PEOPLE ARE FAR MORE SINCERE AND GOOD-HUMORED AT SPEEDING THEIR PARTING GUESTS THAN ON MEETING THEM."
—ANTON CHEKHOV, THE KISS

☾

TAKING LEAVE

Do I really need to pay attention to what time the party is supposed to end? YES! You really do! If the party has been called for 6:00 to 8:00 P.M., and a glance at your watch tells you it's 8:10, thank the host and get the hell out of there. Do not be embarrassed to be the first to leave! Your host, who of course is far too polite to ever say, okay, dudes, the party's over, will be silently thanking you, thanking you, thanking you, for starting the movement.

This is an interesting point, because with most other types of parties, the opposite holds true—your host, most of his work finished, often *wants* you to stay as long as possible. But the preparation for a cocktail party can be an exhausting ordeal lasting over two or three days, *plus* your host has continued working through the party (even if it doesn't look like it), and he will have to clean up when it is over. Besides that, the number of hors d'oeuvres has been carefully planned—not too few, not too many—and whether or not *you* are hungry,

DO SEND A THANK-YOU
NOTE OR FAX, OR LEAVE A
THANK-YOU MESSAGE ON
THE ANSWERING MACHINE.

☾

you can be sure that your hosts probably are, and that they would like nothing more than to plop down in front of a relaxing dinner, probably in a restaurant. And this doesn't forbid you from inviting your hosts out to dinner, although if they decline, just accept it, as they may be so exhausted that they want to be alone. All of this adds up to the tenth and final cocktail party rule:

RULE #10: EVERYONE MUST LEAVE BY THE APPOINTED HOUR.

And although it's not required, it's nice to send a postcard, or fax a note, or leave a thank-you message on their answering machine the next day. They've gone to an awful lot of trouble, and it's really the only decent thing to do, or else they'll worry that you had a terrible time.

TROUBLESHOOTING:

In Which Everything That Can
Go Wrong Does Go Wrong

People have *on occasion* thrown cocktail parties where everything went perfectly smoothly. But more often than not, some little annoying thing will pop up to hoodwink your easy entertaining. In fact, if you start thinking about how many different things *could* go wrong, you might change your mind about having a cocktail party altogether!

But no need to become an alarmist, for the only *real* problems come when you can't see a solution for a problem that does rear its ugly head. Fortunately, there are a number of preventive measures you can take so that many potential problems never have the opportunity to develop, and you'll be assured a calamity-free cocktail party.

A BROKEN VASE

P R E V E N T I V E   M E A S U R E S

1. **Buy more liquor than you think you'll need, or have handy the phone number for a liquor store that will deliver on the double.** This will prevent running out of liquor, the oil which keeps the cocktail party engine running smoothly.

2. **Make one extra batch (30–40 pieces) of some type of hors d'oeuvres, and keep it on reserve in the back of the refrigerator.** Don't plan to serve them; they're really only in case of extra guests or hors d'oeuvres burned while reheating. If you don't ruin the ones you planned nor have extra guests, serve them at your own peril, since guests who have eaten a lot of hors d'oeuvres will not be hungry for dinner, and therefore will have no incentive to leave—ever! If you don't use them, eat them the next day for lunch or dinner, or freeze them.

3. **Keep a few packages of cocktail rye and pumpernickel in the pantry, a couple of packages of store-bought puff-pastry bouchées, and a jar of anchovies.** For many recipes, you may wind up with a little extra filling, or leftover flavored butter, or what have you, and if you keep these "vehicles" handy, you can use your ingenuity to whip up a few extra canapés in a pinch—for instance if you burn some hors d'oeuvres *and* you have gate-crashers.

4. **Always keep a batch of some type of reheatable hors d'oeuvre, such as Gruyère Puffs, handy in the

freezer. It's nice to have them around even if you're not having a cocktail party—you can always pull out a few and re-heat them in the toaster oven as a surprise hors d'oeuvre to serve with a predinner aperitif—and then if you're caught short while you *are* having a cocktail party, you have a five-minute emergency hors d'oeuvre. Notice a recurring theme here? While you don't want to *serve* more than necessary, it's dreadful to run out.

5. Remove any small valuables from the party room and the bathroom, and put them somewhere safe. Of course you know your friends, but maybe you have a friend who isn't *really* your friend. And what about the guests of your friends and business acquaintances? And possible gate-crashers? Sadly, kleptomaniacs *do* exist—and think of it: they have to be *someone's* friends . . . Personally, I never would have thought it possible that a guest of mine might purloin any-thing, but one time I hosted a dinner party, and I knew all eight guests very well (or so I thought). The next morning, I found that several things were missing—a couple pieces of flatware and some personal items from the bathroom. Since it wasn't anything valuable, I had to deduce there was a klep-tomaniac in the house. The mystery remains to this day. . . . Anyway, if it can happen to me, it can happen to you—so do stash away valuables and trinkets of which you are exceed-ingly fond—including items of personal value, even if they're not "worth" much.

6. If you have any "interesting" prescription drugs in your medicine chest, stash those somewhere as well. How many times have you seen a movie or read a book in which someone's guest goes through the medicine chest, perhaps even swallowing some stuff? Maybe this is a myth of popular culture. But why take any chances?

7. **Place plenty of ashtrays around the party room.** If you are permitting smoking, plenty of ashtrays will prevent not only the unpleasant sight of cigarettes crushed out in glasses and houseplants; it may also save your furniture or carpet from a burn caused by someone's ash dropping while they search for an ashtray—it could even prevent a fire. Maybe it could even prevent a forest fire!

8. **Keep a small, home-size fire extinguisher, and know where it is.** This is the kind of advice I can dish out, but would probably never follow, because I'm not that clear-headed type of person. But it doesn't mean it isn't a good idea! If you do keep one, and a tray of hors d'oeuvres or one of your guests catches fire, it can turn a potential disaster into a hilarious mishap!

9. **When extending the invitations, make it very clear that the cocktail party will be of finite duration, say 6 to 8 P.M., and dinner will not be served.** This will prevent guests from staying too late. You may not realize it now, but you *will* be exhausted by the time the party has gone on two hours—after all, you've done a lot of work to prepare. Believe me, you will want them to go away at that point.

10. This one is a really good idea, and I hope you have the nerve to do it. **Let your guests know ahead of time that you have to be somewhere at 9 P.M. Even if it's *not* true!** There are lots of things you can invent—you have to

HORS D'OEUVRES CATCH FIRE

have dinner with someone who couldn't make it to the party, you have to go see a friend who's doing a poetry reading, you have to pick up the kids from the baby-sitter—it doesn't matter what it is. That way, at 8:30 you can say, "Gee, I'm sorry—I have to kick you out so I can go . . .", and you have the irrefutable excuse already set up!

A COMPENDIUM OF TROUBLES

Now that you've done everything you can to prevent mishaps from occurring at your cocktail party, let's grit our teeth and take a look at what you should do if certain dreadful things *do* happen in spite of all your precautions. This could be scary, so maybe you'd better mix up a martini while you ponder the list.

Problem: Guests show up early.

Solution: First, try to understand that your early guests will be much more embarrassed than you are, which is as it should be, because unless you're the closest of friends, it's a cardinal cocktail party sin to arrive before the appointed hour. If you want to take the gracious approach, exclaim, "Oh, heavens—my watch must have stopped!" Show the offending guest into the party room, hand him a drink, and resume preparations, saying, "I won't be but a minute." Your guest may talk to you as you finish your last-minute tasks if you wish, or relax in the living room. In any case, you're not responsible for entertaining him until the cocktail hour.

Problem: A guest arrives on time, but you're not ready yet.

Solution: Basically, handle it the same way as above, but you'll have to strike a much more apologetic attitude. Anyway, the others will arrive shortly, so your guest won't be by herself too long. Hand her a drink, and go put on your lipstick.

Problem: A blizzard strikes.

Solution: Maybe no one will show up, but at least you'll have food and drink to sustain you and your loved ones for a few days!

Problem: It's raining cats and dogs. What if my guests stay home with their cats and dogs?

Solution: Those of weak constitution will, so the ranks may be thinned out to include only the intrepid. Find something to use as an umbrella stand—a plastic wastebasket works nicely—and leave it by the door, along with several towels. Be prepared to reduce the number of hors d'oeuvres you bring out in case of a lot of no-shows, otherwise those who have shown up will stay forever.

Problem: Your boss's husband is flirting shamelessly with someone who's not your boss.

Solution: Though it's not exactly your problem, if they have a huge fight later about his behavior at *your* cocktail party, your boss may subconsciously blame you, and take it out on you in dreadful ways. The best thing to do is to introduce another player into their little tête-à-tête—one who you think will appeal to the woman your boss's husband is flirting with. This is a tricky maneuver, however, because you don't want the boss's husband to turn against you either. Subtlety and tact are key.

Problem: An unruly/drunken guest.

Solution: If she's drunk, take her by the hand into another room, say "Damn—you're going to have a whopper of a hangover tomorrow," and hand her a big glass of mineral water. If she's just unruly, say to her in your best schoolteacher/baby-sitter voice, "Don't you want to be invited back *next time?*" If that doesn't work, surreptitiously call her a cab, and when it arrives, say, "Oh, Bernadette—your cab is here." If she says she didn't call one, insist that she must have!

Problem: A guest who has drunk too much insists on driving home.

Solution: Get your hands on his or her car keys. If it's a woman, this will be easier, as the keys will probably be in her pocketbook. If it's a man, you may have to do a little pickpocket routine, whereby you give him a good bump to create a distraction, and that's when you grab the keys. (If he's very drunk, he won't even notice it.) Pretend like you've let him win, but when he looks for his car keys, he won't find them! Call him a cab, or ask someone sober to drive him, and assure him that you'll find his keys when you're cleaning up. If his house keys are attached to his car keys, and another guest is dropping him off, give that person the overindulger's keys, so

AN UNRULY, DRUNKEN GUEST

265

she can return them when she drops him off. Otherwise, you'll "find" them the minute he leaves in the cab, and he can return for his car and his keys the next day.

Problem: Gate-crashers.

Solution: Make them feel welcome, offer them a drink, and see if you can't ascertain who they are. If they seem okay, adopt a bighearted party spirit and welcome them with open arms. If the finger food seems a little thin, pretend like you don't see the gate-crashers on one or two passes of the hors d'oeuvres—or better yet, "accidentally" skip over the rascals who told them about the party. If you know the crashers and purposely didn't invite them because you don't like them, smile when you greet them, and say, "Oh, you should have let me know you were coming!" They'll understand the sub-text, which is, "Now I won't have enough hors d'oeuvres, you jerks."

Problem: Your party is called for 6:00 to 8:00 P.M., and a group of guests waltzes in at 7:50.

Solution: When you greet them, act happy to see them, yet a little wistful, and say, "Oh, pooh—the party's nearly over and people are just starting to leave. [Even if they aren't.] But surely you can stay for one drink?" Show no mercy if everyone else has left, and they linger still. Kick them out. Or if you can't muster the nerve, suggest you catch up over dinner—in a restaurant.

Problem: A drunken clod spills a Mai Tai on your white upholstery.

Solution: Spill a little soda water on it right away, and blot; don't rub.

Problem: There's a power failure.

Solution: This is more or less serious depending on the season. In the shorter days of winter, make a great show of lighting lots of candles, and the party will take on a romantic rosy glow. In summertime, light won't be so much a problem. Your CD player will quit, but the whole thing is so dramatic and exciting that it won't matter that you don't have music. And aren't you glad you didn't plan on blender drinks?

Problem: A tray of hors d'oeuvres somehow catches on fire in the kitchen.

Solution: If you equipped yourself with one of those little home fire extinguishers I told you about, here's your chance to see if it works. Otherwise, throw some baking soda on a grease fire. At least if you run out of hors d'oeuvres now, you'll have a legitimate excuse!

Problem: You've oversalted something. Have you ruined the whole batch?

Solution: If it's something you're cooking on the stove, put a few pieces of raw potato in it—they'll absorb the salt. Otherwise, try serving it and see what happens. Since bar food is traditionally salty to incite people to wash it down with more drinks, cocktail party finger food can get away with being pretty salty, too.

Problem: Someone commits an embarrassing faux pas.

CLOD SPILLS A DRINK ONTO WHITE UPHOLSTERY

Solution: Pretend you didn't notice, and do or say something to change the subject immediately, but not too obviously. If *you* were the perpetrator say, "Sorry; just kidding."

Problem: Someone gets sick.

Solution: Take them into the bedroom, see if you can give them an appropriate over-the-counter medication, and pray that it wasn't your hors d'oeuvres.

Problem: Someone chokes and turns blue.

Solution: Execute the Heimlich Maneuver.

Problem: You run out of liquor.

Solution: Call the liquor store and beg them to deliver.

Problem: You run out of hors d'oeuvres, and it's only seven o'clock.

Solution: Heat up some of those emergency hors d'oeuvres you have in the freezer. What's that? You say you don't have any? Then try one of the following.

Take out all your bread, spread with cream cheese and garnish with olives, radishes, carrot slices, capers, or parsley. Or figure out something to flavor butter with—anchovies, herbs, curry powder—anything—whip it together, and spread it on bread, cut out shapes, and use leftover *anything* to garnish. If by some chance you have leftover filling, such as chicken liver mousse, smoked salmon mousse, etc.—you can pipe it onto little bread rounds, or the ready-made bouchées you have stashed away in the pantry.

Problem: Someone sits down, and you're worried it'll start a trend.

Solution: Invent a distraction for the perpetrator—something across the room you have to show her, someone standing across the room you're dying for her to meet.

Problem: The party was called for 6:00 to 8:00 P.M. It's now 9:30, and five or six entrenched guests are making no sign of getting ready to leave.

Solution: #1: First, put away all the liquor. When the CD ends, don't put a new one on. Under no circumstances should you bring out any hors d'oeuvres at this point. Wait five minutes and see what happens.

If nothing changes, take off your shoes. Wait five minutes, watching guests closely.

If still nothing changes, put on your bathrobe—they'll get the idea.

Solution #2: Invite them to stay for a slide show of your last vacation. They'll suddenly remember a root canal appointment.

Solution #3: Do what my friend Felix does, and say cheerfully, "Okay, everybody, I'm kicking you out now! Anyone who wants to stay and help me clean up is welcome to." (It takes a person with great stores of self-assurance to pull this one off.)

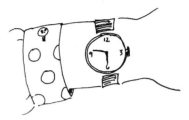

NINE-THIRTY, AND GUESTS
WON'T GO AWAY

9

CALLING IT A NIGHT

It's 8:25, the last lingering guests are just on their way out the door, and the air is suffused with that effervescent after-cocktail-party glow. And a swell party it was, wasn't it? As a good party should do, it built slowly to a peak—the guests chattering away amiably, the music and the cocktails suitably slinky, the hors d'oeuvres accessible yet elegant—and when it crested, about an hour and a half later, it maintained its energetic buzz until eight o'clock or so, when guests began to say their good-byes, and then drifted—happy from good conversation, satisfied from relaxing libations, appetite pleasantly piqued—outward into the evening and off to dinner.

At this point, having been on your feet for several hours, you'll probably collapse onto the sofa—don't forget to remove the pointy architectural replicas—and muse over the evening's events. If you've given the party with your spouse, significant other, or bosom buddy, you'll want to do a postmortem (no cocktail party is complete without one). But maybe we should do that over dinner—you always love that cozy Italian place around the corner. . . .

On your way out the door, put away perishables, and wrap up any extra hors d'oeuvres. If you have any opened champagne, stick a spoon in it to keep it bubbly, and put it in the fridge.

Extra-thoughtful guests will send their thanks—informally, of course. A phone call, a message on the answering machine, a postcard are perfect. Or they might send a thank-you by fax! It's easy to scribble a note the next day, just to let you know they haven't forgotten about you already. . . .

And before a week has passed, you'll be amazed to find you've started a trend among your friends: Someone will call and invite *you* to *their* first cocktail party. Take this as you should—as the highest possible compliment your friend could have paid to your own cocktail party.

Vive le Cocktail Party!

"GRATITUDE, IN MOST MEN, IS ONLY A STRONG AND SECRET HOPE OF GREATER FAVORS."
—LA ROCHEFOUCAULD, MAXIMS

☾

BIBLIOGRAPHY

ALLEN, LUCY G. *A Book of Hors d'Oeuvre.* New York: Bramhall House, 1941.

The ABC of Canapés. Mount Vernon, NY: Peter Pauper Press, 1953.

The ABC of Cocktails. Mount Vernon, NY: Peter Pauper Press, 1953.

BEARD, JAMES. *Hors D'Oeuvre and Canapés.* New York: Quill, 1985 (first published 1940).

BRADEN, DONNA R. *Leisure and Entertainment in America.* Dearborn, MI: Henry Ford Museum and Greenfield Village, 1988.

BRASCH, R. *How Did It Begin?: A Study of the Superstitions, Customs, and Strange Habits that Influence our Daily Lives.* New York: David McKay Co., Inc., 1965.

BURKE, HARMAN BURNEY (BARNEY BURKE). *Burke's Complete*

Cocktail & Drinking Recipes with Recipes for Food Bits for the Cocktail Hour. New York: Books, Inc. 1936.

BURROS, MARIAN, AND LOIS LEVINE. *Come for Cocktails, Stay for Supper.* New York: The Macmillan Co., 1970.

CASTLE, CORALIE, AND BARBARA LAWRENCE. *Hors D'oeuvre Etc.* San Francisco: 101 Productions, 1973.

CHILD, JULIA, AND SIMONE BECK. *Mastering the Art of French Cooking,* Vol. Two. New York: Borzoi Books, 1970.

CLAIBORNE, CRAIG. *Elements of Etiquette: A Guide to Table Manners in an Imperfect World.* New York: William Morrow and Co., Inc., 1992.

The Club Cocktail Party Book. Hartford, CT: G.F. Heublein & Bro., 1941.

Cocktails as Served at the Hotel Martinique, New York City. New York: American Hotels Corp., 1938.

COLLINS, PHILIP. *The Art of the Cocktail: 100 Classic Cocktail Recipes.* San Francisco: Chronicle Books, 1992.

DEVOTO, BERNARD. *The Hour.* Boston: Houghton Mifflin Co., 1951 (first published 1948).

DUFFY, PATRICK GAVIN, *The Official Mixer's Manual: The Standard Guide for Professional & Amateur Bartenders Throughout the World.* Garden City, NY: Garden City Books, 1956 (first published 1940).

Editors of *Esquire,* with Scottie and Ronnie Welch. *Esquire Party Book.* New York: Esquire, in association with Harper & Row, 1965 (first published 1935.)

Editors of Time-Life Books. *Hors d'Oeuvre.* Alexandria, VA: Time-Life Books, 1982 (first published 1980).

Editors of Time-Life Books. *Snacks & Sandwiches*. Alexandria, VA: Time-Life Books, 1980.

Editors of Time-Life Books. *This Fabulous Century*. 5 vols. Alexandria, VA: Time-Life Books, 1987 (originally published 1969).

ELIOT, T. S. *The Cocktail Party*. San Diego: Harcourt Brace Jovanovich, 1978.

ESCOFFIER, AUGUSTE. *The Escoffier Cookbook: A Guide to the Fine Art of French Cuisine*. New York: Crown Publishers, Inc., 1969.

Esquire's Handbook for Hosts. New York: Grosset & Dunlap, 1953 (first published 1949).

Gilbey's Recipes for Cocktails & Other Mixed Drinks. London: W. & A. Gilbey, Ltd., 1934.

GRIMES, WILLIAM. *Straight Up or On the Rocks: A Cultural History of American Drink*. New York: Simon & Schuster, 1993.

GURNEY, A. R. *The Cocktail Hour and Two Other Plays: Another Antigone and The Perfect Party*. New York: Plume, 1989.

KAFKA, BARBARA. *Party Food: Small & Savory*. New York: William Morrow and Co., Inc., 1992.

KAROFF, BARBARA. *South American Cooking: Foods & Feasts From the New World*. Reading, MA: Aris Books, 1989.

Mr. Boston Deluxe Official Bartender's Guide. Boston: Mr. Boston Distiller Corp., 1974 (first published 1935).

RIDGEWELL, JENNY. *The Book of Cocktails*. Los Angeles: HP Books, 1986.

ROMBAUER, IRMA S., AND MARION ROMBAUER BECKER. *Joy*

of Cooking. Indianapolis: Bobbs-Merrill Co., Inc., 1953 and 1975 editions.

TOUSSAINT-SAMAT, MAGUELONNE. *History of Food.* Trans. Anthea Bell. Cambridge, MA: Blackwell Reference, 1992.

TRADER VIC. *Trader Vic's Bartender's Guide, Revised.* Garden City, NY.: Doubleday & Co., Inc. 1972 (first published 1947).

TRADER VIC. *Trader Vic's Book of Food & Drink.* Garden City, NY: Doubleday & Co., Inc., 1946.

TYRER, POLLY. *Just a Bite.* New York: Prentice Hall Press, 1986.

WILLIAMS, CHUCK, GENERAL EDITOR, AND THE SCOTTO SISTERS, RECIPES. *Hors d'Oeuvres & Appetizers.* New York: Time-Life Books, 1992.

INDEX

Entries in *italics* refer to recipes.